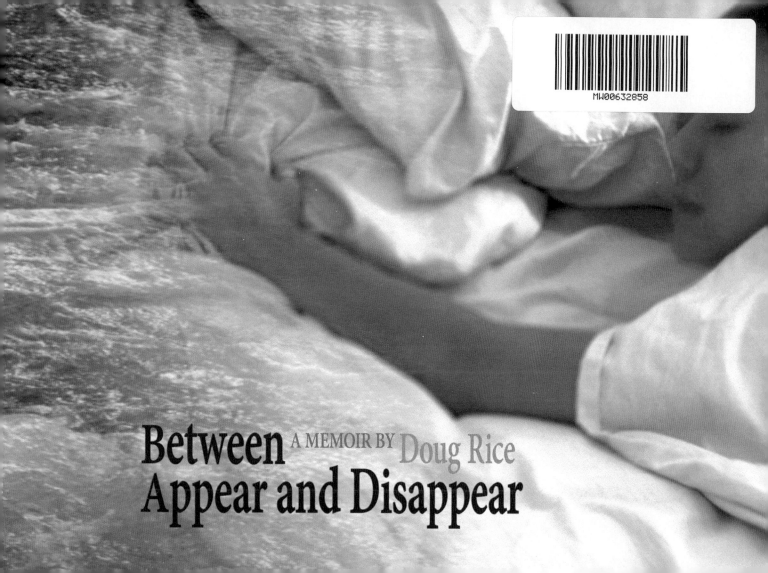

Between A MEMOIR BY Doug Rice
Appear and Disappear

Between Appear and Disappear

A MEMOIR BY **Doug Rice**

Jaded Ibis Press
sustainable literature by digital means™
an imprint of Jaded Ibis Productions U.S.A.

© 2013 copyright Doug Rice

First edition. All rights reserved.

ISBN: 978-1-937543-06-8

Library of Congress Control Number: 2012936451

Printed in the United States of America. No part of this book may be used or reproduced in any manner whatsoever without written permission from the publisher, except in the case of brief quotations embodied in critical articles and reviews. For information please email: questions@jadedibisproductions.com

Published by Jaded Ibis Press, *sustainable literature by digital means*™ An imprint of Jaded Ibis Productions, LLC, Seattle, WA USA

Cover and interior photography by Doug Rice. Cover design by Debra Di Blasi.

This book is available in multiple editions and formats. Visit our website for more information: http://jadedibisproductions.com

This book was not so much written by Doug Rice; rather, it was written as a gift for a woman whose name remains silent with dreams, a remembrance of moments of breath and of skin near rivers.

Acknowledgements

Not without my children: Cory Douglas, Anna Livia, Quentin Joyce.

Not without Jordan Okumura. Not without Lan Do-Nelson, Don Harrold, Tess Perez, Vicki Pearson-Rounds.

Not without Kathy Acker, Carole Maso, Trinh T. Minh-ha, Helene Cixous, Theresa Hak Kyung Cha, Anne Carson, Francesca Woodman, Luce Irigaray, Jean-Luc Godard, Wim Wenders, Clarice Lispector, Derek Jarman, Gilles Deleuze, Frida Kahlo, Peter Greenaway, Marguerite Duras. And not without Debra DiBlasi.

Not without Lotus. Not without the South Fork of the American River. Not without those rivers coming to a point in Pittsburgh.

Never without this deep bone-memory and this stillness. Never without Beauty.

For an abandoned myth.
(I write to you.)

But first it is necessary to leave.

(So as) never to arrive.
The third that walked beside Mai and Doug erased something that can never be erased.

We spoke near to our desires. Elsewhere. Within here.
Mai's words waited inside this silence for a moment then evaporated into water.

(Once, and once only, Mai whispered, "What I've wanted to say, I've perhaps said.")

My mouth near the dew of her thigh.

This morning prayer, this breath of silence, this literal translation of Mai's tears into the water of desire.
The never of always.

The simple forgery of Mai forgetting to tell her one story of loss.

On waking, we found a ruined mirror that had been abandoned along the South Fork of the American River. A mirror decayed by years of use. Our bodies had become so secret that this mirror refused to reflect our skin near to each other, near to breath, near to dreaming, near to touch.

(The anatomy of our longing vanishes. In rain. In morning. In snow.)

The true subject of any photograph, you must continually remind yourself is not there, is not the visible that you merely think you see but the invisible: what has been repressed and what will not be written. Mai traveled with me to the invisible, to the invisible that is here. The invisible that remains within.

Beneath this photograph on the inside looking the other way (in the tain of the mirror) are traces of a desire that has been worn out. "Mai's body beneath this photograph was removed on August 6, 2011." What role did photography play in this remembrance of time past? (I am told, have been told, my tenses are always wrong, were always wrong before the present moment. That, like Benjy, I can never control past and present. Still she remains. And commas disappear at inappropriate moments. Impermanent permanence.) Remembering destroys memory and creates a fugitive memory, an eclipse of desire. Mai became an orphan to the lens, to the frame, to the moment.

"Truth," Mai always dreamt of saying, "is the thing, the longing, you must not say." Known and unknown mourning for a volatile and impossible tongue. Between absence and presence. "And is that love?" I asked her. "What does it matter, love, a word."

Because memory is inside there. Eaten by the light.

No less alone than a poem.

Sometimes, beneath blankets, beneath quilts, beneath stars and moon, beneath the writing of this sentence, the loved one is erased. Words entangle her body in memories. Her touch disguised beneath letters descending blindly into the throat of the night.

"I don't know if I am going into your dreams, or you into mine."

But Mai's memory began there in the small breath of a child surrounded by fireflies and falling stars.

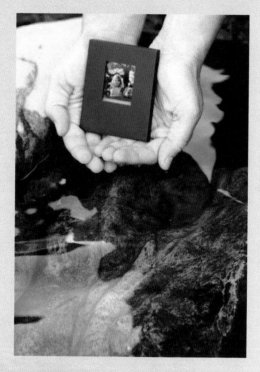

That loss of meaning. That impossible name.

Every photograph poses itself as this one question: Are we allowed to view what is being exposed?

Inside each photograph there are tiny pebbles, tiny grains of stories from the old country. Childhood memories of mouth and of tongue. Childhood moments of telling stories of breath and of rivers and of dakini girls beneath blue moonlight in the foothills have so much power over our hearts because they hold the secrets of who we were then and of who we are now when we reach across the silence, across the years, between words, between worlds, to touch.

Mai took photographs of sentences she had abandoned in childhood.
She took photographs of words before words became water.

I think we may have feared mistaking the beginning for something else.

We found it nearly impossible to say anything believable in a sentence. There were too many knots.

"At the sound of your voice, you are here."

"*Here* is the secret name of your presence in my soul, in my heart, in my muscle, in my breath."

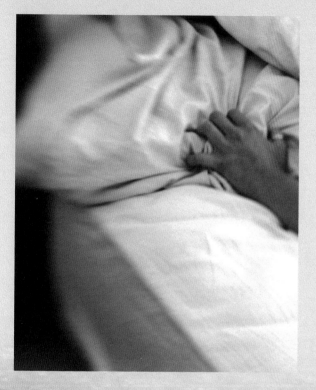

At best, the most terrible truth of any photograph is that it can only show us what happened; it is forever trapped by the past tense. Photographs can never show us what is happening or what will happen. They are always imagining something that has already disappeared. Always. Forever already disappeared.

It is you wanting and knowing to wait. How to. Wait. She wanted.

This photograph is the remains of that which is gone. Of that desire. Of that hope. Of that story. Of this love becoming a myth, abandoned there along the river.

First person narratives can never be translated, they can barely be written. Such ways for telling stories can only be spoken in doorways, in shadows, around corners. And they can only be heard for this one moment. Then she will forget that such stories had ever been told.

Writing "I" tends to remove her from these stories.

Our desire creates its own displacement. The fabric is torn.

"Can it be so wrong," Mai writes from her bed in her home miles away from electricity, away from light.
"Can it be so wrong to write to you knowing that one never does what one wants?"

From Tijuana, Kathy wrote sentences on the back of religious postcards. She wrote each word of each sentence to the point of delirium. A small Frenchman in a narrow street in Paris had whispered secrets to her. Secrets that could only be repeated as scars. She sat near me in a grey café in Alphabet City, attentively watching for what happened to my flesh when I read her new manuscript. The closed lips of her words.

When trapped by the stories of her ancestors, Mai turned herself foreign. Her tongue in the mirror. Her speech in Vietnamese, in French, in English. Veiled.

She encountered my mouth and translated my silence into the sensations of her body.

"I'm going to tell you a secret: *chaque fois que je dis je I je jette un coup d'oeil autour de moi poru voir ou* You is."

True translation always, of necessity, reveals its own foreignness.

I see only her trace between wax and wane.

Her breath.

Remains in my mouth.

Not even this sentence becomes any more true because of the presence of the I, nor is it any less true given the limits of this I. My body always slips the moment before becoming her desire.

This life of my body writing your I is a synthesis of multiple dreamscapes. I dream of you in the snow. I dream of you across the ocean in deserts, in jungles, in cities.

"My hand," Mai scribbles across the back of a postcard with a photo whose image is so faded that it can only be mistaken for something other than what it is. "My hand is in your hand which is in my hand."

In a desert Mai's skin itches. Burns. Her eyes want to see.

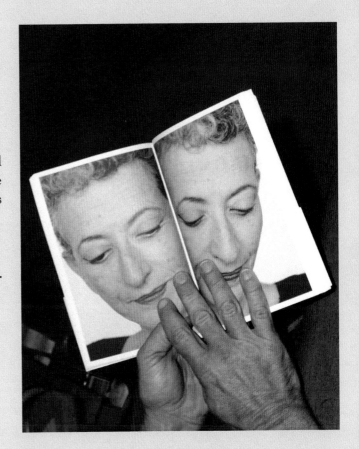

In the end,

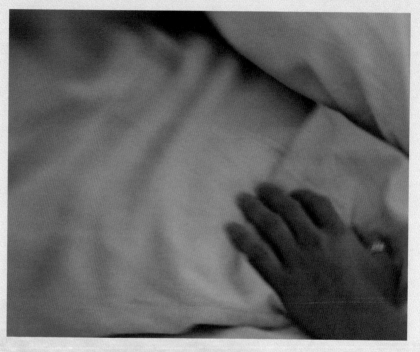

we had nothing to be mysterious about. The sheets damp with tears, damp with desire, damp with sweat, damp with lovemaking, damp with dreams.

But to see. But to touch. But to write. Beneath stones along the river. We must unlie.

In dreams, water syllables rested beneath her eyelids.

Mai carried me to that first place, that moment without memory.

This uneasy negotiation near the touch of our origins. The framed desire of this image. Wanting. Longing.

Written words are always waiting. On skin. Beneath river water.

The current writes Mai's desire into her dreams. Stealing pleasures. Her only rest is motion. To go where she has not yet arrived. Already photographed. Lips in movement on skin. There is a veil. In solitude. There is a caress. In stillness. There is a waiting.

Mai struggles to experience the place of words in her body. The slow patience of her tongue, of her lips. The care she gives to each letter, the way each letter shapes her mouth. Each word changes her. This foreign tongue she now speaks as if it were her mother tongue.

J'ai toujours aime l'eau passionnement.

Mai tortures words. Teases them with tender slips of her tongue. She only speaks around the edges of letters. Innocent, yet punished like trees after a torrential rain and windstorm. Ripped from their place of stillness.

Beneath her language another language haunts her. One more agile, one more ancient, one more elusive. She tells me that words from these places can barely be spoken. This is the language of our lungs, a breath that pries open our lips. Qu' est-ce qu'une priere? Climbing mountains in Vietnam, Mai walked on the bones of her ancestors. Each footstep over the dry earth, the rocks, she felt her ancestors cry.

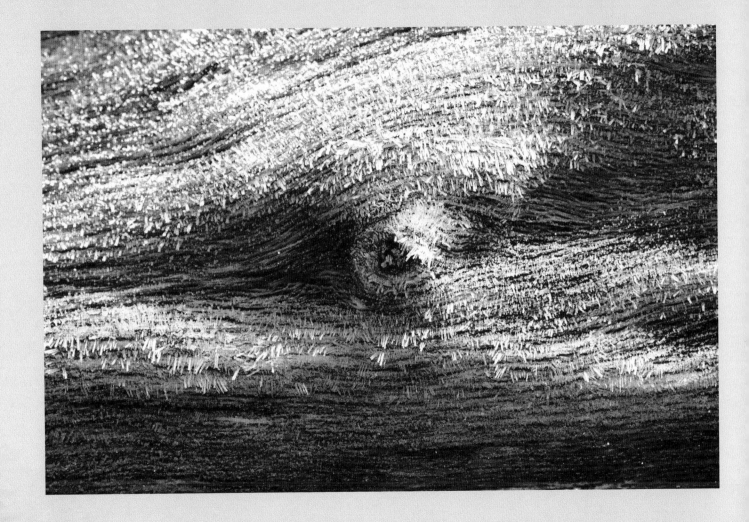

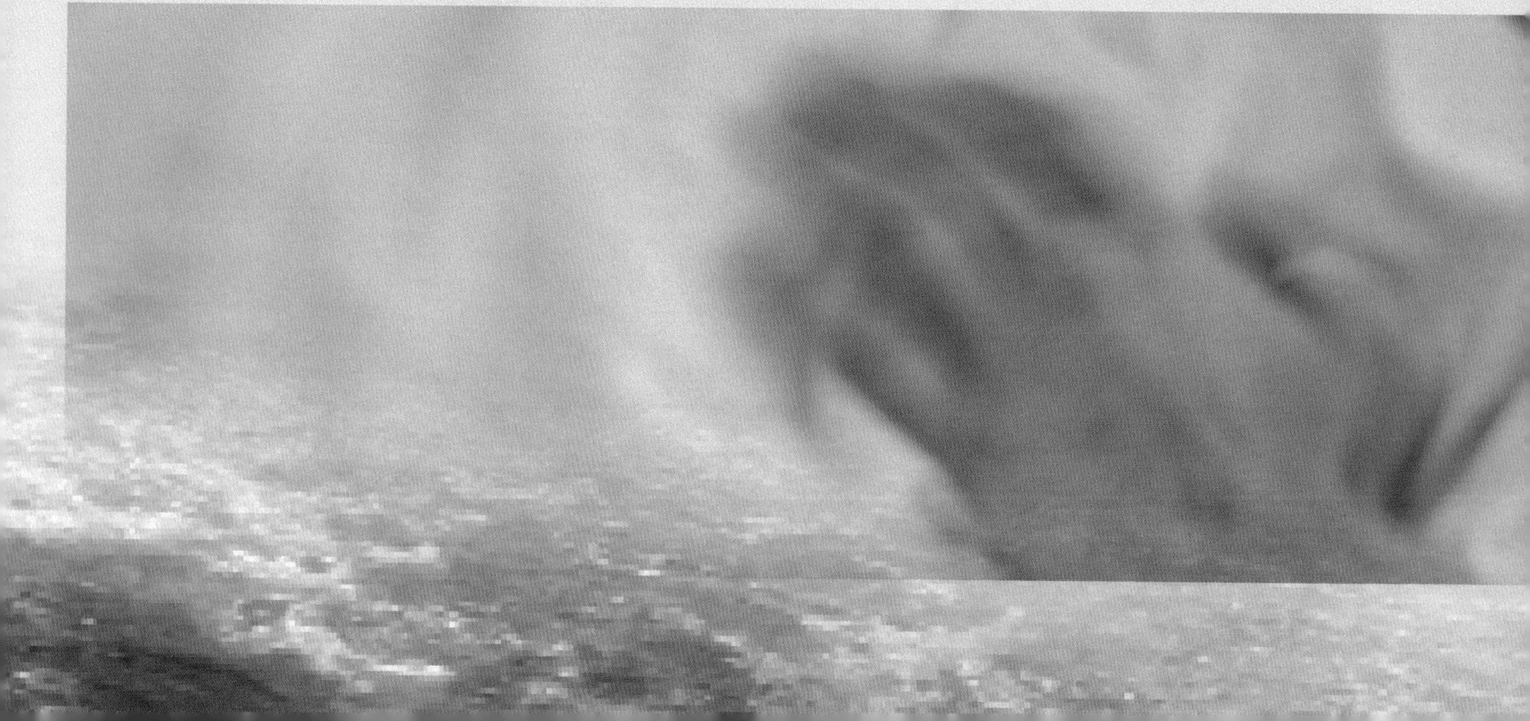

A frozen lake one day before the first spring thaw.

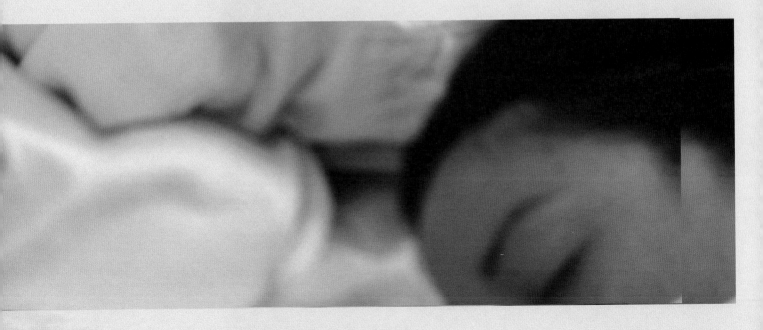

"But, for her, none of this is sacred."

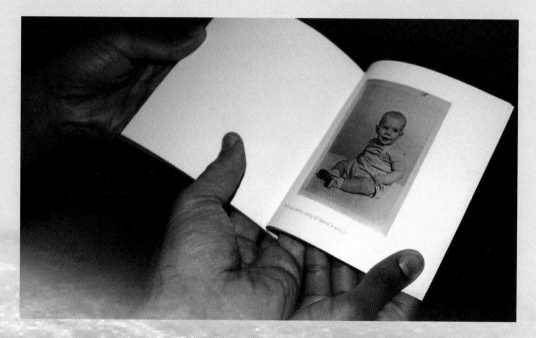

Mai touches in disbelief a child's writing. Bare legs streaked by cold air. The wet ground. In the center of her palm, she holds a vague desire to understand. A moment when tears turned into words.

One wants what one cannot want to desire. Stories of her childhood have been lost in these rivers. "You continue to forget." Give, yourself, desires.

Nothing is ever more tempting than temptation.

Mai's lonely fingers teased the surface of the water.

What is written is not said.

At her table, Mai sits, hunched over, writing. Scribbling. Making so much noise that I cannot hear the crickets or the tree frogs in the yard.

I watch her hands working on the page. Her shoulder muscles and her biceps making poems. Making visions into words. Forming desire out of words detached for only a brief moment from her breath, from her skin. Mai's willingness to write is so strong that she nearly writes through the paper down into the center of the earth. And Mai only writes with a pencil. The lead from her pencil covers her fingers, her knuckles. She rubs out as many words as she writes. Her words always on the verge of being erased. Words written on top of words. Words crossed out. Many of her words are missing. They have been lifted off the pages and rubbed onto her skin. The words that do remain on these pages, in these poems, carry her skin with them.

She looks over her shoulder at me. "I'm writing fake poems," she tells me. "Make-believe poems. The kind you can put on paper. The kind you can turn in for grades. The kind other poets read." Then she smiles and goes back at it. Real poems always get lost before they arrive. Orphaned moments of tranquility.

At dusk she erases every syllable of these fake poems.

"Don't use a comma. Ever. Promise."

Once upon a time, in a gentle fairy tale, two estranged wayfarers discovered, scribbled between sentences meant to carry the reader safely to an epiphany, a wild fuck that abandons hope.

In these days of living in a dry land that wants fire, we need to find words, or burn.

Last night we dreamt of rain. Mai standing near my skin, on the bank of the American River, her flesh wet with simplicity. The scent of star thistle mixed in with river mud. "I meet people in my dreams who have never known the inside of a lotus flower. Ever." In the center of each word another word unfolded. Our ankles cold from the river. Her hands trembled. Bewildered fingers.

Photographs should be wet. Always. Wet. Always.

The nostalgia in these photographs is rarely visible except to the vigilant viewer, the spectator who stands still, who peeks through the folds, who maintains a devotion to patience.

Mai and I crossed into each other's languages. Obeying only those words that haunted us.

Tongue.

Finger.

Lips.

The brail of this loving.

The tips of Mai's fingers as precise, as agile, as an eyelid.

"I only wish to dominate desire."

Be careful around those who claim to know the history of fire and yet remain unafraid of rain.

Mai steps closer to the edge of the river, her body nearly falls.

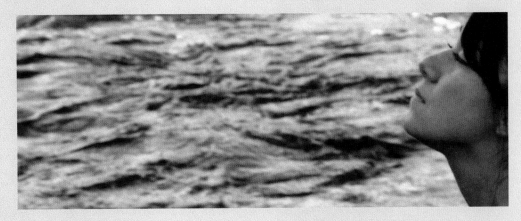

"All through the foothills of Vietnam," she tells Doug, "there are people whose skin is made of rain."

Mai's body waits for the sun to vanish behind the clouds. Her fingers childish and curious pulling blackberries from a bush. "Some say such people are only the people of myth, of old stories dropped along the way, the wet underside of river rocks." Her eyes witness the appearance of these words, her words, her breath, her dreaming. "These people say this as if myths are not true, as if the people of myths are not real. But I have met these people. I have touched the water of their skin. I have listened to their damp voices, their whispers, their murmuring sentences."

"Who is this this?"

"Khong biet sau nay tui no con nho tieng me de khong?"

Once upon a time, we are told a story of a day before the war ended. She says, "You see only her trace." He says, "You have not forgotten enough."

This woman remembered the fear more than the pain. And she remembered the blackberry bushes cutting into her ankles more than the pain that she knows she will never speak of.

She screamed at this pain, screamed against this pain, screamed into this pain to make it go away but it never went away. Ever. Even now. Even in this moment.

Imagine a butterfly being pinned to a board. That tiny cry of terror suffocated beneath glass.

Some man blindfolds this woman then pushes her down into the mud. She does all she can to remember that day long ago before those bombs began falling down on her village, before they dug tunnels, before they learned this new way for breathing. She does all she can to remember that day she picked herself up out of the earth.

She imagines she is made of water.

Then someone with soft hands, a young girl perhaps, undresses this woman. The woman listens to the child's soft crying as this child unbuttons what remains of this woman's blouse. The woman wants to comfort the child, to whisper a prayer, a chant with her voice, but this woman can no longer speak. Her tongue has been burned by coals.

This woman moves her fingers to lightly touch this child's hair to let the child know that there is always hope, that trees reach up from the earth to touch the sky.

Naked.

The child's touch abandons this woman.

Callused hands grab the woman's wrists, pull them behind her back. Binds them with rope.

Nineteen years of innocence but now this woman's fingers break. Now her wrists burn. Now her strong tongue touches the roof of her dry silent mouth.

Maybe so she will not forget, she falls asleep.

Mai contemplates her wounds. Only damaged skin can seduce her body. Torn flesh. She cuts straight lines across her wrists. She cuts as deep as she can so each cut became a scar. Most memories remain silent. Siren songs to herself.

When she spoke of home, Mai tasted fires on her tongue. Her words turned to ash.

She wept. On her knees. At the river.

Mai thought it possible to photograph silence.

Only silence is chaste. "Why do you want so much to speak? To begin there?"

The blood of Mai's ancestors ran through her syllables. Her mother, when Mai was still an infant, warned Mai that if she ever bit into her tongue, she could poison herself with her past, the stories from before she was born. But Mai thought biting her tongue would release the stories of her ancestors into her body, into her desire. So she bit and bit until the blood from her bleeding appeared.

Her tongue, heavy, swollen with centuries of words, of wounds, of sacrificial petals from the Lotus flower, bled into her voice.

Mai speaks confusing tender words, prattles in tongues that war against each other—the home tongue of her grandmother bombed to pieces by this tongue she has adopted in exile.

Mutilated words made out of the bones of her ancestors fall from Mai's lips.

Her loose hair surrounded by butterflies.

Have you ever stepped into a tremor with your tongue?

I never understood that water has roots until I listened to Mai talk of her home.

Each syllable, a moment of sound filled with hope. A magical breath giving birth to Mai's desire to remember the days when words surprised her mouth with the joy that comes from having discovered new sounds. Most of her life she had been obsessed with this need to recall the very first time she ever heard a word, to bring back the exact order and sound of each letter and how these sounds made meaning possible. She said the inside of her mouth enjoyed saying metempsychosis nearly as much it enjoyed saying ineluctable modality of the visible.

"Some words," Mai told me, "exist for no other purpose than to be said aloud, to be whispered into the darkness when you are alone and wanting nothing more than to experience the longing of your body to escape the ashes of this life. Kind of like sugar on your tongue. Words of this nature wait for us to arrive; they lurk in distant shadows. It is as if they come to us and in a gentle way they disturb those false promises that we are prone to believe. The kinds of promises—pacts with the devil or with God or with parents or with the mall—that we are afraid to question because we are so fearful of what we might discover about our own identity."

Mai sat on the cold cold bamboo floor of our home in the foothills outside Sacramento, rocking back and forth, chanting words that were nearly impenetrable. Words with twisted letters and disturbing etymologies. She rooted around her memory for those words that she found curious for no other reason than for the way that they felt as they moved through her body until she released them out into the world. She put her body to work, used her body, to rehearse these words before planting them onto the page. She forced her body to fully experience each word before she allowed them to join her poems. Words remained with Mai.

"Close to my womb," she said, "the way rocks remain in rivers."

Words and rocks both carried similar markings from the physical wearing away of time. The trauma a rock experienced was visible on its surface and this trauma shaped the rock; in this same way, a word is marked by the trauma it experiences while being remembered by our bodies. Words had places of origin and of home on the inside of Mai's desires. She sheltered them. They sheltered her. Each word carried geographical and geological histories of the whole of Mai's life from the inside out. Words, for Mai, were never simply one-dimensional flat inscriptions on paper or utterances that disappeared.

Words were not those casual marks made out of letters that people found in dictionaries. When she was young, so young that she laughed at the most perfectly inappropriate moments, Mai began setting fire to dictionaries. "They're not words, Mother," Mai complained. "They are faking it. I can't let people see words in this way. I can't let people think that this," she held the charred remains of a dictionary up in front of her mother's disappointed eyes, "that this is all there is to a word. That this flimsy thing is their home." Mai came close to crying. "This," she shook the dictionary, rattled the skeletal remains of the words, "this, Mother, is a tomb."

Mai still burns dictionaries. Burnt my only dictionary a few years back. She said it was for my own good. Set fire to it in the bathtub. Said she was protecting me from lies, the kinds of words that people only used for crossword puzzles and for afternoon tea on some estate far out in the countryside of dear dirty France.

No word but stones.

"Con nghi phai hoa minh voi ngon ngu thi moi duy tri duoc tieng me de."

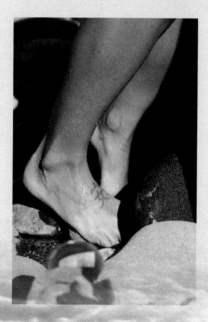

Mai tells me of photographs that can only be seen by remembering them.

"I touch your rain soaked wounds in secret."

Each sentence as it is written is written to create silence, to lead us to a place of silence. The silence that follows each sentence should endure as long as it has taken you to read the sentence. This silence is different from white space. This silence should fill your body, not simply remain on the page. Your body needs to experience this silence. The duration of this silence cannot simply be reduced to the white space of a page, to external marks. Silence needs to mark you.

These mirrors that appear in these photographs are always something other than what the words suggest.

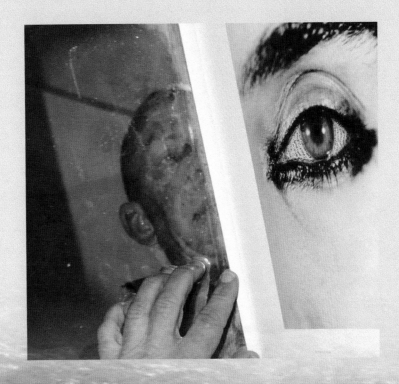

In the middle of a lonely sentence an unknown woman turns up, then vanishes.

I am missing words for this sentence.

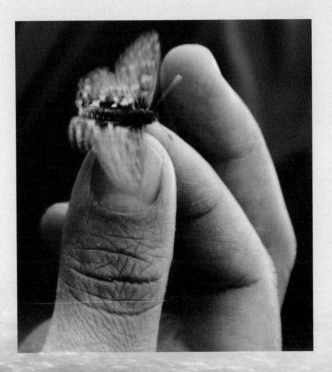

A sentence, Mai once told me, cannot come to this. Not now. Not ever.

Speaking in the tongue of her mother, Mai's soft voice became the song of a sparrow lost among tree branches. Other women from those same hills in Binh Dinh spoke in the tender spirit of butterfly wings. Veiled whispers beneath quilts. The need to survive in quiet movements. The longing to continue their stories. Each story one of flight through the trees to the plains, to the rivers, to the oceans. In the loud streets of San Francisco, people ridicule her gentle voice, a voice that releases words with such care that the air remains still around her mouth. They say her savage mouth will never understand their language. Her teachers demand that she speak like a human. Children in her class place boats made out of newspapers on her tiny school desk. It is darker than any darkness when her family pushes their unsteady boat into the water. Inside this darkness, they fear lighting their bamboo lanterns, and when their eyes close to sleep, to dream, to collapse, they are haunted by a fear that they will live inside this darkness for the rest of their lives. This water, all this water, this ocean, all this water must end, but her family, so quiet, can no longer find their faith, only splinters in their fingers and these persistent small pains in their strong feet. They want to disappear beyond the dark night, fall off some unknown horizon. And they fear arriving as much as they fear drowning. They speak to each other through the whispered songs of those nearly forgotten sparrows so their voices are not heard. Ever. They dream the only dream they can remember, a dream of becoming birds, spirit birds nearly invisible in the night sky, more dangerous than dreams. In some other world, far away, where such birds cannot be heard, where birds are not listened to, an uncle, holding paper names tight in a small fist, waits on dry land.

When she opened her mouth to tell these stories of her family, the air filled with butterflies.

Mai's skin is moist, her voice damp. Always. And never the opposite.

Ashes and water.

Mai dreamt with her tongue.

Pomegranate seeds between her teeth.

Persimmon flesh between her fingers.

Between.

Her knees held tight.

Her thighs bruised and tired.
A stray thumb near her lips
Presses.
There is nothing in between.
A thumbprint.

Stains.

When does a photograph begin to make sense again?

Her fingers remember the time before and she comes close to speaking in signs, in wonder, in touch, in light, in water.

Water obeys water.

"I look at you as at the passage of the word into flesh, of the flesh into word, a lasting incarnation, a bridge toward a becoming that is yours, mine, and ours. Together we gaze upon the invisible. A perception toward the not seen. I look at you, love you and think of you but what I perceive, love and think about is not mine. There, here, now. I participate in your gaze. While becoming me, I remember you."

She could no longer recognize the rain from her dreams from the rivers from our breath.

Je ne peux pas te toucher sans que tu me touches.

Speech, for Mai, was always a battle with language, for language, over language, into languages. She held words in her mouth, lingered with them, tended to them. Her eyes nearly coming to tears with this holding of her breath. She did not withhold words so much as stayed with them so that she could more fully deepen her experience of each word, of what they might have to say to her as much as to those to whom she spoke. She wanted her words to always remain, to carry these remains with her.

Others rushed their words out into the world as if their words had no origins, no body, no place in their memory with their memory. As if words were as silent as the space waiting for words.

When Mai and I spoke, we spoke in spite of words, in spite of silence.

Mai wanted to enter into mute spaces.

Mai became quiet, the lost thread of some vague longing near her lips.
A desire to unravel the riddle of trying to speak clearly.

Before the photograph remembers, there is loss.

Or if only for a moment. If only we could return to the gaze we knew as children.
Hold our breath and close our eyes and wait for paradise.

A girl carries her body through jungles across deserts along rivers down empty streets.
A blind hunger for touch. Your tongue in me. It was just physical. Not an emotion.

Little worlds—land with water everywhere, land with dakini girls—
the tiniest grain of sand pressed like skin prayers between Mai and me.

In the mail a broken letter arrives and I am reminded of life before stillness, of life before Mai, a life before the foothills, before solitude, before silence. And my body aches with this elsewhere for these birds that have gone mad and emptied the river of water.

It's five a.m., Julia writes from Brooklyn, and I live here above some kind of shop that sells everything that will never be fixed. It's like being in one of Paul's novels. And my meds are sitting in their tiny white bottles waiting but they don't know how to laugh or when to laugh. They never get it right. Little round bits of silence. These will make you quiet, the kind doctor told me. When I put one on my tongue and swallow, the whole world turns into soft vowels and each lonely world turns greenish blue and even the taxi cab drivers are quiet and it snows even in July.

Julia says she has conquered time but not distance. She says her roommate, Judy, is no longer her lover, just her roommate, and it doesn't feel right. It never feels right. Not any more. Will it ever feel right again? When will it feel right? And now Judy is inside a globe on a bookshelf and she simply refuses to come out. It is snowing inside the globe and Judy appears to be surrounded by water. There is sadness in every corner of my apartment and there are symbolist poems mixed in with cat hair scattered all over the carpet and the vacuum is broken. Even when I dream lonely lonely lonely for you, she writes, I can't fully understand your legs in that lovely dress. I miss your writing, but I know it in me like blood. That rope tied to a tree. Abandoned. My thighs red and quivering. I'm a lucky girl. I am unable to remember why I am writing this sentence, unable to write or to think or to remember. I think I just wrote that sentence. I am unable to remember how to write this sentence, any sentence. My mind is just a vapor. Your tongue is a red unfurling anesthetic. I miss it. Give it to me.

Her sentences disappeared into the page. Fading away. Her pencil becoming weak or tired.

This page has suffered. Take it out in the rain.

"In the morning," Mai says, "I want to write a sentence that besieges your flesh.
A sentence from which there is no escape."

Mai rubs.

She rubs words off my skin. The world becomes a solitary place with the first rainfall of autumn.

Mai told Doug the Vietnamese legend of a story that never begins. A story that waits the way a flower waits to bloom. A story that waits the way an old man waits for a blade of grass to grow. With this same patience, Mai waits before she touches the world around her.

She spoke each word as if it were the very first time or the very last time she would ever say it.

"I have found," Mai writes from Viet Nam, "islands of silence in the forests."

The way migrating birds hesitate.

The way light slips through the branches of scrub oaks.

Mai carries words, old as rain, tattooed on her skin. Speaks in the rhythms of breath and water. This forgetting of air. She lifts her toes from the river water. "In the beginning," she says, and quickly smiles over at me, knowing that I am thinking of her as my Buddhist poet, my beautiful Lotus flower inventing beginnings out of shiny, pleasure domes of ice. "In the beginning," she begins again, "words are physical sounds, vibrations without a path. The birthplace of words intrigues me in the same way that a dream of a lover—a lover who will only be born through a desire for home— haunts me. Words cause muscles to spasm with desire as they pass through my body, over my flesh like white water over green rocks. Later, words become pictures inside dreams and thoughts. When spoken with care, when words are tended to, words become concrete moments of faith for those absent desires that have fled far up into the foothills away from these corrupt cities. Near the last of their breath, words finally may, under certain light, at specific times of day, communicate a longing. But before all this, before all these beginnings that have been named, that have been scripted into biblical myths, words began as fossils. Eventually these fossil words become rooted in the soil of our infant silence and we have forgotten them. We live our lives forgetting and forgetting until we disappear in the noise without taking time to enter the silence of being near to each other's bodies. The roots of all words are little more than mythological threads, a way for carrying the past into the present, to this moment and to this place, here and now. These roots travel back to their places of origins where a word was in the beginning a fossil."

"Repeat a word too often," Doug continues, "and it will leave scars in you. Sacred tears that years later will fall from your eyes. Repeating words is like skinning your knees over and over on concrete. Words possess this kind of intimate and destructive power, a power to skin."

Even as shadows made their way across her bedroom walls and left their scent on the spot where once there was a mirror, she remained chaste.

Mai stopped talking. She held onto her breath and touched the very corner of her mouth.

Like a mirror, a photograph both invites and denies touch.

When I erase, I erase carefully so as not to tear the paper, so as not to make the original words disappear. Over time these very faint ghostly lines of flight surface as evidence of an other beginning. Birth marks.

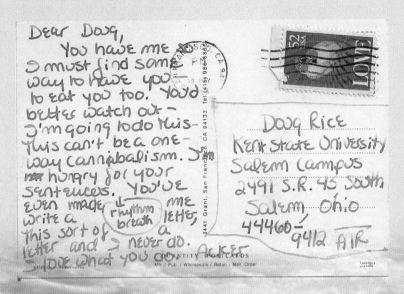

I write sentences, even this sentence on top of dead sentences from the past, a past that never fades. In memoriam to identity. I turned architecture into a verb. And I write on top of that past that is never forgotten, that past that is never past. Through the suggestions of these barely visible traces, the residue of the past held to the present. Past desires and possibilities lingered in these visual echoes.

I want to touch this shadow. Here.

In fire, words become cinders. They wait for fertilizing rains.

Every photograph is a fetish.

(…a fetish to keep an eye on.)

True books always contain one sentence that appears to be a secret.

Those years above the Lotus Valley. "I love to you." That was our one sentence then. This is another sentence. A shadow crawls up and enters your heart. It's not so much the words themselves and what they might mean; it's their shape. The weight in my body. The way a word makes my mouth feel. The taste of an ancient, well-worn word.

Years later on Nob Hill in San Francisco, I would become silent with wanting my hand to write what my heart felt, to plant words to the moonlight. Who can say the word "love" when our pale and elegant memories disappear in the vapor of daily living? She feels a tiny bruise rising purple and strange on her dark skin. Moonlit butterflies outside her windowpane. She wanted him to look at her without caution.

This sentence waits. This is the sentence that will always wait and will never appear. This sentence is the one that longs for a moment near your dark skin. In Stuttgart. In Lotus. Near the South Fork of the American River. In Solitude. Along the edge of the Presidio. This. Sentence. That. Lingers. She held in the palm of her hand a pebble the color of moonlight. Her beauty rested in the movement of her desires, of her deep, strong laughter. A sweet drowsiness spread through her muscles. She escaped sentences. Always. To love what you will love because there is nothing else to love. Thin as air. Rounding her mouth, she let out a tiny scream. This sound cracked her dry lips. Surprised her breathing. Opened her muscles in stillness. A moment of longing before waiting. Moist. "That sound," she whispered into my ear, "that sound should be kept secret." She put her fingers over her lips.

Her mother refuses.

Imagine your hands are naked. Truly naked, not just bare hands but naked hands. Skin. Muscle. Blood. Memory.

Imagine it has been raining for weeks, for months, for years, raining for so many days that you cannot remember your skin ever being dry.

Imagine digging into mud with your naked, naked hands.

Imagine while digging into this mud, digging this hole, you sing the only lullaby you can remember from your own childhood, from the songs of your mother, from the tunnels beneath the earth.

Imagine a child lying on her back beside you in this cold, cold mud.

Motionless

Silent.

Imagine this tiny child staring into the sky. Waiting. This tiny daughter of your flesh, of your blood.

Imagine this tiny tiny child waiting. Waiting for you to dig this hole into the mud with your naked, naked hands.

Imagine you cannot dig the hole deep enough. You are too hungry. Your fingers are too broken. Imagine you are too weak to lift this child's body.

Imagine you were the one who survived and found a narrow boat and a river, and a way to escape into the dark night.

Imagine God did this to you. Imagine God forced you to be the one to survive.

Imagine this woman, who survived the burying of her first-born daughter, gave birth to another daughter while sleeping in mud in a camp surrounded by barbed wire and a promise, and she took this other daughter to some other land.

Imagine you are cursed with this woman's knowledge of graves.

Imagine at least one person every day for the rest of your life, when they look into your eyes, asks you: "Is there something wrong?"

Imagine you remember this child waking you in the middle of the night.

Imagine the words you speak are heavier than your body.

Imagine you remember this mud even in the dry desert heat of Borrego.

Imagine your body has emptied of everything you once trusted in and believed in as your mother's daughter.

Imagine it remains possible to go on living.

Imagine writing sentence after sentence to the disappeared.

Writing this sentence hides all the other sentences I am not writing.

Remember you are not reading the sentence I have erased in the writing of this sentence.

Through an accidental tear, a few secret sentences do survive.

We fell upon a place where nearness turned to separation.

"There are impossible, illegible, or forbidden narratives: for example, the one I won't tell you."

In our house, mirrors have begun to replace words. We live in silence and occasionally catch a glimpse of our desire for words in reflections before our image disappears. But these moments of seeing that which is not here never endures. A mirror cannot replace the longing for the possibility of a photograph. A mirror can never even be like a photograph; a mirror is too much of time, trapped by the disappearance of the present. And photographs of mirrors are always merely a disappointment, an echo of an impure desire to re-enter the past. This desire to see backwards is doomed to fail from the beginning. No mirror can preserve the past. In fact, mirrors carelessly destroy the past.

I turn my back to this murderous mirrorhand to recover my own memories.
The experience of my life through the mystery of the sentence.

Is this still writing when words enter water?

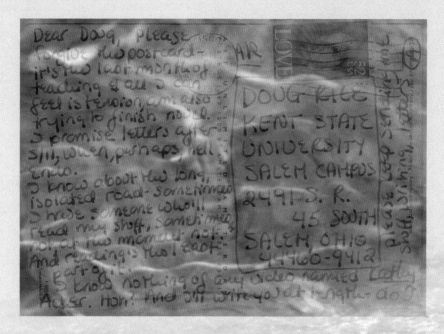

Mai tells me when I write on her skin she feels blue.

The color, not the metaphor.

"Your words," Mai says, "are naked."

Without a trace, Mai disappeared into an unnatural photograph. Her subtle flesh moved through those invisible spaces, the ones that separated here from there. Dark clouds burst open and a spring downpour washed away Mai's faint footsteps. No marks remained of her slightly curious departure. No one, not even Mai, knew where she had been nor where she had arrived. Her flight down into this little passageway is now only remembered inside the language of tidy bedtime stories used by fathers against the desires of their daughters. Stories told before the night falls; stories told in order to keep infant girls locked in childhood innocence. Safe and still. There, and there alone, without ever coming to be here, Mai remained forlorn and sweet. Light forehead kisses like breath over a mirror from forgotten fathers. Unspoken litanies from misbegotten mothers. The helpless bodies of Mai's sisters and of her unborn daughters were tucked inside sheets, frozen beneath the weight of heavy blankets. Girls everywhere being told to sleep tight and to dream well. Princes will charm you with their kisses early in the morning. Dream the dreams you wish to live.

But Mai was not like other little girls who sat quietly at the kitchen table, and she was not like her daughters who waited patiently for her on the inside. Mai feared that if she ever fell asleep she would never again awaken. She worried that she would become stranded in red corridors with billowing white curtains. Crammed with wonders already forbidden, she suffered the joy of being photographed by her dreams of these unborn, unbound daughters. Mai thought that all her infant traveling, which she did while sleeping, would never belong to her. These travels into places without language would only be captured inside the voices of strangers.

Mai lost herself in the impulse of this dream.

This man, the shadow haunting her dreams, had hair on his knuckles and blisters on the very tips of his fingers.

She longed to cry, but she lived in a body without water.

In her mirror, looking, Mai caught herself, a small child of dry tears, suspended between doubts and dreaming.

Her oldest older sister, a lonely girl, pressed her hand on the dark spot of her younger sister's bedroom wall, the place where the mirror used to be. "I am older than you, and must know better." Mai herself was no longer there; she had become absent and could only enter her sister's life through stolen photographs. Torn photographs of broken dolls, of girls with black hair, twisted and matted, of crippled girls with mouths that had been cut open in the belief of a promised land, were scattered everywhere in Mai's memory. Light from these photographs made her eye twitch. Mai's voice became lost in the desert that arrives before looking. Her hand reached out from beyond the past of the missing looking-glass.

At times the terror of her own reflection took over the real. There was no way out of that place, out of the present. This one small trauma had cut into her body and lived there, alive in marks on the inside of her skin. She no longer could look away from her own looking. This gaze of a curious girl in love with bewildering wonder.

Mai had grown tired of eavesdropping. Once upon a time, when she was still a child, she peeped into her sister's books, but these books were always without a quiet place for looking. Now Mai had slipped, a sudden accident, into the inside of one of these nearly impossible books. A hopeless book without dialogue. Readers rubbed their fingers over her breathing. The bread crumb trails of her words. Drawn and quartered photographs from the land of broken sins. Readers following and following their own longing to turn the page, to see Mai, like Alice, growing bigger and bigger and smaller and smaller. She never was one to remain still. With each touch she changed. Abrasions of her skin were torn from her body as she disappeared into the lonely palace of language. Still, she left shreds of paper, fallen leaves from mimosa trees, for her sister to follow. To cling.

"Come to me when I am not looking."

Mai grew exhausted by the lonely stares of those old men she had read about in Alice's letters. These abandoned strangers who drifted down the River Isis beneath Nuncham Bridge. Their picnic baskets overflowing with cakes and tea. She wanted to always be safe from such strangers hiding behind trees.

"In a small cottage, I posed and I became exposed," Mai read in Alice's notebooks. "I recall experiencing a mysterious thrill gazing up at my own shape emerging from a negative clipped to a string. Day after day, I watched myself in the darkroom of Charles' stories."

Mai searched for ways to escape truth and to avoid guilt, so she sewed words beneath the hem of her dress, and she smiled and twisted her body into playful moments that broke the trust of those watching her. "I just wanted to be a happy girl who refused to be really frightened." Mai sought uncertainty and wanted to transform her skin from the reflection of others' desires into her own speech. She tried to look to the inside of time. She caught on the other side of the mirror a glimpse of her sister or Alice or Alice's sister reading a book that appeared and disappeared.

"This is the photograph you stole," she whispered to her older sister, "and you are the woman. I am becoming."

Mai feared that Alice never believed in herself beyond the wooden frame of her looking-glass.

Alice often warned Mai about men who lived their lives under the cover of false names. She slapped Mai's wrists. On her lap, Mai's older sister held books. Opened books with pages and pages of ink. Spilled desires. She rarely ever lifted her eyes away from the stream of words. Mai stood beside her sister with her hand resting on her shoulder. She watched her sister wet the tip of her index finger and turn another page. The words turned into mirrors turned into rabbit holes turned into decks of cards. Without looking away from her book, Mai's sister spoke.

"Be careful around the outside of mirrors, Mai."

"You may fall in."

Looking-glass deceptions threatened to become flesh before the word. From the insides of the book, Alice told Mai stories of other tiny girls who had been cut to pieces by broken glass. "You're living there," Alice said, "as unfinished, as perishable as a flower." Mai wondered about her sister's reflection. The one she saw once, a long time ago, in her sister's vanity.

Mai began dreaming to be here before the eyes of her victims. To remain not yet a woman of her own. In her mirror, a girl once surprised Mai into looking away from her own body. Mai held this girl by her hand until she became invisible and unknown.

"When was the last time you recognized yourself?"

Mai waited.

She followed Alice along a trail inviting nomadic men from diseased homelands to look into her, to grow suspicious of their own desires. These men loved to stare at her with their frenzied eyes. Her opened mouth transformed into a kind of benediction. The moment before prayers. She wanted to trap each of those men, to force each one to stare back into their own reflections. Mai wished to violate their eyes with her body. To be captured in the gaze by the purveyors of the plague. Each morning sitting beside Alice, she awaited the stares of these men with their derelict mouths and desperate hands. Men who pinned her to the tain of the mirror. A paused image that stuttered near the tremble of knowing. They told her lies while she squirmed. They did not know that Mai knew these were the lies of greedy men in despair. They told her that dirty knees were the sign of an innocent girl. She, because she knew what could not be said, shifted her weight from one hip to the other. Her mouth had edges. They took first one photograph of her skin, then another. Photograph after photograph of her gaping wounds. She lived in this world of photographs without end.

"I can only see what I've already seen."

Like a photograph whose images continue to emerge.

Mai fell asleep reading Alice's diaries. In Charles Dodgson's great, quadrangle study, she saw Alice become an archive of still-life photographs. Stolen images of skin and hope. Portraits and reflections. Frozen and framed by the trap and release of a shutter. Image after image fractured. No longer an outside. She longed to find her way to be on the inside. Away from the deprivation of looking. Here, Mai waited for a witness. One who could escape to tell what she had seen. "Tell me one story," she pleaded, "that is not afraid of truth." These men, standing before Alice, tiny Alice's gaze, their hands stuffed deep inside their pockets, became guilty. Charles had written on Alice's eyes with desires that did not belong to her. Mai feared that all of her life would be condemned and surrendered to the inside of one of these silent books. One without drawings. She tore her sister's books into pieces at the very moment when Alice was not looking. She thought these deaf and dumb books would murder her daughters before they could be born. She wanted simply to wash Alice's eyes with water from the river.

"You are no longer there, Mai."

"Here."

She remained in silence, existed simply as this incompletion of words, wanted only to live on the inside of time before the making possible of forgetting. She carried with her untold stories. This weight of memories. Ghosts that haunted her. She could not name these ghosts from her past. Wished only to speak one sentence to her sister. But her mouth hesitated. Not one single memory of her childhood could break free. She longed for her own echo to call to her. Desired a way to travel with Alice back into the shadow behind Charles' mirror. Her refraction broken and upside down.

Mai wanted to stay beneath the inside of sleep. To be covered by the dead petals of her nearly lost memories. "Wake up, Mai dear!" Her sister's distant voice from a far-off-land. Mai lingered, remained a moment with her dreams. Remembering her own child-life, she whispered back from her long sleep and carried her sister with her to the place before sacrifice. There, she found the sound of her own voice.

Shadows never leave scars no matter where they touch you. It is as if the shadow never touched your skin to begin with, as if the shadow were only an apparition. The same is true of mirrors. No visible traces of looking are left behind. Your eyes remain innocent, unmarked.

She slept as if she had never been born.

\\\

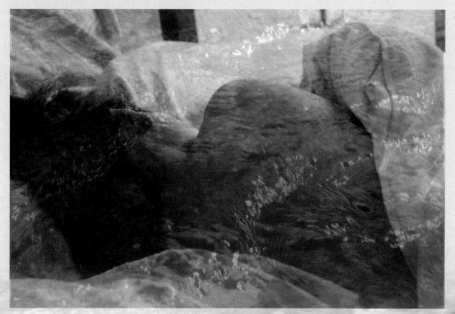

Like the sound of eyelids closing to dream.

All photographic images risk being transformed into myth. Stories of lost remembering. Haunted desires for a world that has vanished into dreams. This past December I found, by accident, a photograph of Gaby and me at the Middle Fork of the American River. Her fingers grasping my forearms, my fingers holding onto her elbows. We were guiding each other over river rocks, neither of us aware that my friend Don was photographing us. We were simply there with each other inside that moment, the cold water washing over our ankles. Holding to each other. Balancing our bodies on the slippery rocks. I had forgotten about this photograph until I stumbled over it. This broken return. While the existence of this photograph had slipped from my memory, that moment of being with Gaby has never left my body. Once, Mai told me that she never wanted, even by accident, to look back at our relationship through still moments captured by film. "Our bodies will remember for us."

Photographs of Mai are rare. No photographs of her early life exist. She said that her mother had not even snapped a single baby photograph, and when the hospital staff came to Mai's mother and showed her the newborn photographs of Mai, Mai's mother said, "I'll take the baby instead." And her mother left the photographs in the hospital. The only photographs Mai had of her life were of her experiences in the world but none of them included her. No traces of Mai.

I sat on the floor in the old home up in Cool with Gaby. Packing. Sorting through photographs of other people and making the connections with these photos to the stories I had told her. Illustrations for all those nights spent talking. Stories and pictures. But none of Mai and none of Kathy Acker either. Years back, Matias Viegner and I were on my front porch in Salem, Ohio, talking about Kathy. Neither of us had ever taken a photograph of her. Not one. "I just never thought she would ever leave," I told Matias. "I just trusted that Kathy would live forever and that her friendship would always be right here with me." But Kathy did die. A month before I was to visit her in

San Diego. I told Don I would return with photographs. Bring back pictures. But Kathy died before I could get on the plane. Before I could arrive at her bedside. The ovarian cancer moving so fast. Her last phone call ended with her promising she would wait. That she was fine. The herbs, she told me, were moving the cancer away. "I'll wait for you, Doug." Kathy's voice on my answering-machine. And she whispered in that light girl voice of hers, fragile with hope, "I am exhausted from writing all these books of pain. Let's promise to write happy books." Then she died. And she died without photographs. And there was nothing that could be done. Not even a photograph could save her.

Now everyone who touches my skin touches Kathy. Gaby once asked me if I regretted. If I wished for one photograph of us. I looked at her lips, the shape of her mouth, and I knew I would never forget. A friend of mine told me he didn't believe that I actually knew Kathy and spent time with her. "You don't have any photographs of the two of you together," he said. "How do you expect me to believe you? I would've taken pictures."

Gaby and I hiked so many miles, so many trails through the foothills down into the canyon, while we were together. We both wore out two pairs of hiking boots. Took so many photographs of the rivers, of the hills, of the trees, of the skies, of sunsets, of everything all around us, but rarely did we ever take photos of each other. Perhaps because I thought she would always be in my eyes. Mitzuko in Jim Jarmusch's film *Mystery Train* asks her boyfriend, Jun, why he only takes photographs of the insides of hotel rooms. He tells her he only photographs things he knows he will forget. He tells her he will never forget being outside and he will never forget being with her. Photographs tend to cling to an already disappearing possibility and desire.

Mai wanted Doug to keep an eye on her. She stood near a tree. Her skin close to the bark. Naked. Without touching. Looking.

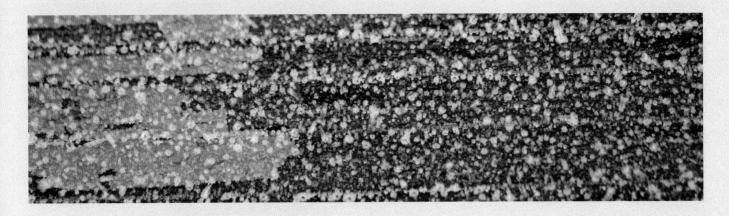

This reflection accidentally caught by a flash of light created a space between awareness and longing. Still, she refused to appear. From outside the frame, she called in words, words not meant to be heard, words meant only to be seen. Perhaps a photograph can only turn moments of unnerving beauty into a sense of the just missed, the nearly arrived.

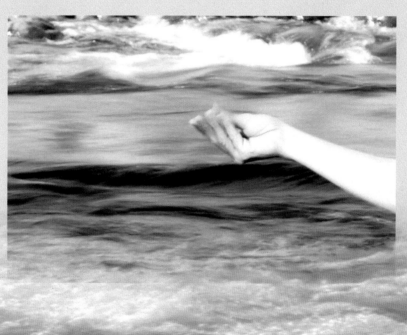

This love of you.

The Secret Book of Twelve Moments
As listened to by Doug Rice
As written for Mai

Twelve words wait for Mai beneath the skin of my left wrist.

Mai scribbles awkward poems that recall a world before the hinges broke. She refuses to read or write the final couplet of any sonnet. She sings uncertain villanelles that are eager with longing to melt snow. She writes careful odes onto tiny pebbles and fears their dreamlike truth. She erases unaccented syllables because her body does not fully experience them. Mai fills in white space with dirt and roots, flowers and twigs. To make reading more dangerous, she ends each line with star thistle. In that moment before sunrise, she breaks her poems open on rocks. Sitting near a window, she dreams of wordless poems made from moonlight. In the distance, twelve harmless butterflies interrupt Mai's poem then fly away. Leaving her pencil on her writing tablet, Mai follows their flight. She longs to touch the space between the wings of each butterfly.

Twelve words can rarely be spoken in a single breath of air.

"These words, whispered to you here, sound like they are only stories." The rain that fell from orange skies burned into my grandmother's skin. Beneath the earth, in narrow tunnels, Grandmother sang to her young daughters. Legends of girls, whose skin made of soft raindrops, survived the bombs. Instead of teaching history, history should be rubbed deep into our muscles. The fury of a mother trying to sew her child back together. Old women weeping like gnarled children over the bodies of dead infants. Night after night, my ancestors were destroyed by your naïve, polluted history. On television, men in white shirts praised the repeated bombings of villages. History can never tell the stories of this mud between Grandmother's toes. For many years, the earth above where Grandmother lived was never quiet. One day, my grandmother simply stopped talking and stared out her window.

Twelve twilights wait in silence for the river to move more slowly.

Mai lit a stick of myrtle incense near the White Lotus River. Grey lines of smoke rose and disappeared into the dark night sky. Scented prayers floating toward old temples in the hills of Viet Nam. Mai was silent with her breath, with her hope, waiting for memories. Ants carrying messages from the bowels of the earth troubled her toes. Canadian geese skidding across the surface of the river broke the silence. Even in moments of migration, Mai promised to be faithful to memory. She told stories of a father who cut down a persimmon tree. She whispered of the sorrow of a young child who never slept. With a tongue of ash, she prayed over her father's lonely dreams.

Twelve sentences are written where once there was only hope and desire.

Mai buried what she dare not forget under rocks at the river. But this river could not cure the loneliness locked inside her body. She longed to touch her shadow, to protect her shadow from fires. More than drowning, shadows, even river shadows, feared the uncertainty of fire. Mythical tongues and crooked teeth, lips and saliva and desire, thuy tinh. The spirit of this water rescued Mai's quiet shadow from lost memories. "You need to place pebbles on your tongue to understand my words." A droplet of cool rainwater slipped from the tips of Mai's fingers. The river, riddled by her memories, haunted the roots of her sentences. Slowly, Mai began to unweave those blurred childhood fables beneath her life. Changed into water by secret rivers, she lived life within ancestral voices. Her tongue loosens, her fingers stretch, she speaks languages rooted in mud.

Twelve losses: memory, language, belief, trust, skin, wonder, desire, hope, muscle, touch.

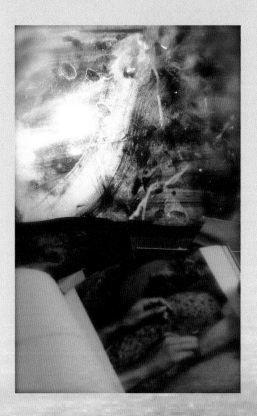

Mai's name, when spoken by careless, foreign
tongues, becomes only a sound. I believe this is what
the word invisible must mean: abandoned breath.
Late one night, Mai hiked through snow-covered
trails to my doorstep. The house surrendered its
silence and she entered the narrow, cold rooms.
Moonlight vanished from the bamboo floor and
we were alone in stillness. I no longer remembered
the sentence I was writing before Mai arrived. If
we are not careful, this becomes the place where
we vanish. We moved our bodies toward each
other, interrupting our solitude with silence. I did
not know we were on our way to becoming exiles.
Her curious fingers drawing small rivers and trees
on nearly innocent paper. We wanted to write
sentences that rested near the possibility of truth.
Now, in her absence, my words, my sentences will
always remain unfinished.

144

Twelve unfinished, illegible sentences waited in that hour between dog and wolf.

"You have not forgotten enough to truly see into your own memories." Mai did not understand what the architect meant when he said this. Beneath the morning light, his skin and her skin covered by ashes. Wrapped in white sheets, their naked flesh scarred by fury and sorrow. Mai wanted to know the original etymological relationship between forgetting and forgiving. Tiny French books suggested that forgetting and forgiving are related to gifts. But she feared she desired so deeply that she would never forgive. Each memory a journey into a time and a place without maps. Mai imagined sentences beneath her eyelids, sentences that formed painful, enchanting litanies. She longed to undo each of these sentences letter by unbelieving letter. Mai arrived at a surprising place where she could no longer write. Her next sentence, patient, waited for the believing that travels beyond belief.

We lived inside the wilderness of a sentence that refuses to end.

The subtle curve of Mai's words made from dirt, made from stone. From the bark of lonely pomegranate trees, she carved ancient, muddied words. She cut fairytales from the fruit of these trees, their innocent seeds. Red, wet letters scrawled across her dark skin dreaming of weeping rivers. Mai refused to form the breath of her sentences merely from words. She mixed the pulp of pomegranates with the insides of lotus flowers. She learned those secret ways for writing on the surfaces of water. Onto the whitewater of the American River, Mai scribbled these lost words. A diary of her innocent travels up and down green mountain trails. Familial stories of water written directly from her tongue, her parched lips. She carried each of these stories beneath her skin, near her womb. And she listened while she wrote sentence after sentence onto the rivers.

Mai longed for twelve moonlit sentences to play with her dark hair.

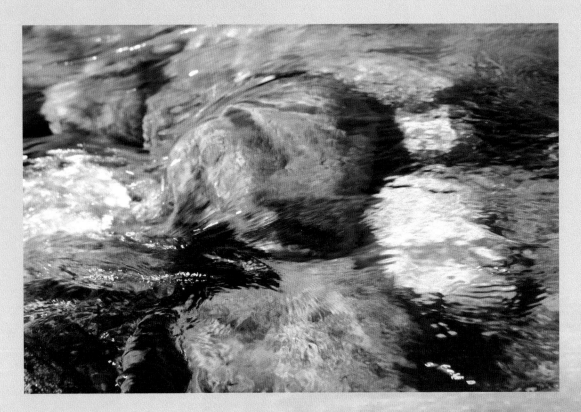

Mai's tongue, her throat, her bones, her muscles, her feet, her skin. She shaped her words, rooted in water, through desires for raw beginnings. Mai pulled word after word from beneath her silent and still tongue. A few words occasionally burned her lips before she could say them. The earthly branches of her roughened syllables moistened by careful morning rain. To write, Mai only needed to feel the breath of her body. The language and longing of her lungs, of her womb and ribs. Where her body is most tender, Mai wrote one word in pencil. She copied all of her memories onto the seams of her clothes. With each step, memories rubbed against her flesh, awakened her tender muscles. While I slept, she hid words carrying her memories beneath my fingernails. Her slender fingers, smooth as river stones, smelled of garlic and lemongrass.

Twelve tattoos on Mai's back tell the true story of that night.

We found the most beautiful sentences imaginable beneath rocks in the river. Endless sentences written by the branches of trees weeping over the whitewater. Mai said these rocks and trees had been ripped from her bones. Inside these rocks, these trees, she saw the myths of her youth. After the moon rose above the mountains, she grew quiet, almost naked. The river reflected the harvest moon and she said her childhood came rushing back. In our garden, Mai washed her hands with rosemary, mint and rain. Between her fingertips, she rubbed two raindrops together and smiled. Mai said she could never explain this water falling from her laughter. This water that told stories from the inside of her waking dreams. She feared those stories hidden behind our eyes would someday become visible. Words that our mouths had caressed, words that had enchanted our lips.

Twelve times Mai told me this story that I can never tell.

Then this one night, the one night that cannot be forgotten, arrives. This night that can never be forgiven breaks open Mai's fragile heart. This night of loss continues, to this day, to burn her fingertips. She carries each breath of rain from that night on her skin. But for this one night, the autumn rain had always been innocent. In her sleep, her muscles, her joints, her dreams, her prayers, remember. She is reminded of her promise, of her barefooted prayer on pavement. Every waking moment covered in tears, in rain, in mud, in hunger. This night sleeps in her body the way rivers sleep under stars. She fears growing old and losing her memory of this one night. In the morning she pulls me toward her with all her strength. She waits for that one dawn when these memories would all stop.

Twelve words disappeared into the river before this book could be written.

Here is the beginning of this story that I can never write. Not even to you beneath moonlight in snow can I speak this. I write words belonging to your story on rocks in the river. At night, the river caresses these words, your words in my hand. By morning, the moonlight and the whitewater have washed away each word. One late summer afternoon in a whisper you told me this story. I remember your fingers tapping the table as you released each word. A little sunlight fell through the oak trees and touched your hair. Your voice vibrated against my skin, your voice moved into my muscles. You spoke of rain; you spoke of broken ribs and of kinship. Then you wrapped your voice in silence, in stillness, and you waited. A butterfly caught by the breeze and blown against a brick wall.

Twelve journeys beneath moonlight, across oceans, over rivers, through jungles, beneath sunlight.

She counts every word in every sentence in every book she reads. "Before this happened to her," Mai says, "I was a young girl." The loss she bore witness to, this loss, she continues to wear. She tells me the past tense has a desire to become present. She remembers the fear of remembering more than the pain of remembering. To write, to unwound, to go beyond the place of family secrets. It is difficult to speak because Mai's tongue gets in the way. As a child, Mai lost three sentences; now she chases night shadows. Mai cried twelve forbidden tears before her memories vanished into the river. No word can describe the silence that surrounded, that ravished her body. The only escape possible is if this sentence somehow went terribly wrong. "What is true is that I want to be alone for once."

In the film version, the screen would quite often turn blue.

The desire in this sentence can only say, or only say again, what already exists in its language.

The rest remains silent.

Mai and I unearthed movement inside the silence where speech existed without a "why"—love because we love, flower because it flowers. Language that is never spoken, except at certain moments prior to thinking. A language that would not desire to be seen or to be heard. A language of longing without return.

And the viewer would have to be patient. The viewer would need to listen.

Only a poet could write of what we saw in these mirrors.

To be drawn into the mystery of a world that seeks its incarnation.

The subtitles in Jean-Luc Godard's *Contempt* appear too quickly. They appear on the screen before the actors actually speak their lines. We know too much too soon. Beauty is erased in such an anxious desire to get it said and to get it seen.

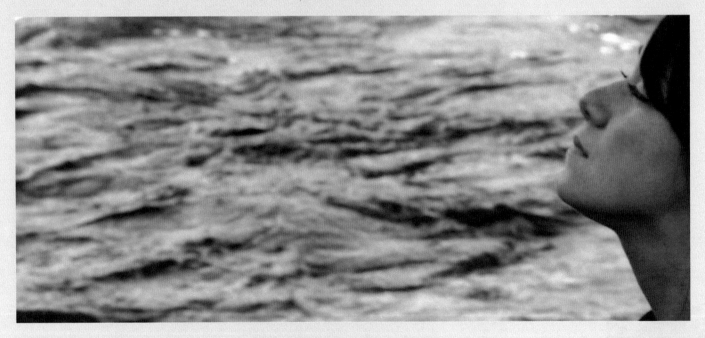

Mai remains on the threshold.

We loved removing each other's clothes patiently the way a hummingbird dances near a flower. I unsnapped Mai's jeans and she unsnapped my jeans. And we smiled. And we told each other epic stories of weaving and unweaving sweaters. And we told each other stories of rivers that had no origins. We told tales to each other of forests where there were no fathers. Then, even more slowly, we pulled down each other's zippers. It was as if we were inventing eternity. Slow, like a seagull taking a single grain of sand from the shore and flying out to the middle of the ocean where the seagull drops that grain of sand, then flies back to the shore to get the next grain of sand and does this again and again and again until the seagull has taken every grain of sand from the shore and put it in the middle of the ocean. We moved toward each other's skin with this slowness. With this attention.

A photograph only suggests an utterance for presence.

Mai pulled a twig from between her lips and gently placed it on the page near the flattest of the pebbles. She looked up at me, then went right back to her stones. "The wet ones are calling," she said. Between placing rocks and pebbles on the page, Mai picked at her knuckles. Stories that clung to her skin from those nearly forgotten days in the hills of Viet Nam, stories that made little girls along the river's edge weep. Watching her play with her skin in this way made me feel irresponsibly innocent.

"A word is merely a shadow of your desire and a shadow never leaves a stain. Your teeth, your knuckles, your collarbone want me in ways that words never will be able to express, that no word will ever come to understand. And your muscles bruise me like a poem, a real poem, one written without fear, one written without regret, one written without metaphors. A poem written to be a poem."

She wanted to flee the one-dimensional world that had trapped her body. She paced around the apartment tearing up books, ripping up her poems. "They're not thick enough," she said as she ripped apart two of her poems. "There's nothing to them. They're afraid of me." And she tore into more of her notebooks. "They don't even resist me. They don't even bite." She picked up a rock and made as if to tear it in half. "See the difference?"

She gave birth to water in her throat.

Mai was filthy every day of her life. Her fingers always got dirty when she wrote poems. Crayon marks on her jeans. Black ink stains on her fingertips, paint on her cheeks, dirt behind her ears, dirt on her knees, mud on the bottoms of her feet, fertilizer on the heel of the palm of her right hand. When Mai wrote, she wrote with every muscle in her body and her body ached as much after writing a poem as it did after a strenuous hike or after a hard morning of lifting weights. There was never anything innocent about Mai writing a poem; the writing of her poems always left stains. "I am a woman," she once told me, "who has been soiled by her writing of poetry."

Mai says she hears echoes in my voice, echoes stained by a love that had disappeared, rivers that had become exhausted and turned dry. Mai was the one who gave birth to water and continues to live in my skin. I never understood that water has roots, is rooted, until I listened to her tell stories of her ancient home far away. Her bare feet, cold and blistered, on dirt floors. Her tiny hands picking delicate fruit from strange trees while her grandfather fished. Even this water of the South Fork, always in movement, never tired, is rooted as it carves its way into the dirt of the banks along the river, trying to remember. Mai and I stand among smooth worn rocks, rocks made round by the winter rains and the muscle of this river straining to come home. In her, the rivers move. Her scent rooted to this movement.

Outside, the moon disappeared behind dark clouds. The snow had begun. By morning we would be snowed in. No electricity. A fire in the woodstove and the quiet world of the foothills slowly being called to life.

Mai's breath fell on ruins.

That's what makes you want to write this sentence.

Along the banks of the South Fork, a true pomegranate is rare. A delicacy. Something that is never to be eaten alone. Mai wet the soil surrounding this one tiny pomegranate with her breath. Words slipped from between her lips, words slipped down into the roots, the movement of the American River.

Somewhere deep in the seeds of the pomegranate, stories of Mai's childhood unraveled. Stories of wolves roaming along the edge of a darkened forest. Stories of candles that can never stay lit. Stories of moons that disappear, of moons that fall into rivers.

On rocks worn smooth by the whitewater, Mai tells Doug the bedtime stories she dreams of one day forgetting. She tells him of time. Of river muscle. Together they wait, between sentences, between commas, for the pomegranate to ripen.

At dusk, Mai places the pomegranate between Doug's knees. He learns patience. When the moon disappears, he is taught to peel away the flesh of the pomegranate.

Days later the pomegranate begins to shrink. To rot. To collapse in on itself. The skin loosens. Clumsy ancestral stories that had been written on the underside of the pomegranate's skin become exposed by the light. Dreams that did not happen that way. Withered curses. Warnings of the furies.

Mai and Doug tempted each other with memories until, exhausted, Mai bit into the pomegranate without leaving a trace.

In the spring, these seeds, the ones that remain from Mai and Doug, are planted. Old stories are turned inside out and comfort the coming of new skins.

Your eyes remain innocent, unmarked.

Mai and I stood barefoot beneath the night sky, pebbles pushing into the soles of our naked feet. Her fingertips near my fingertips. Our absentminded movements slow and careful, attentive to the quiet. We stood in this perfect moonlight, surrounded by falling stars and memories of fireflies, waiting for the snow to begin. With each breath we came close to touching each other but we held our bodies in this stillness.

It is because of your words that I have skin. Your stories return me to the earth. Muscle and bone, the crack of joints. You tell me not to remember your stories. You tell me story after story and beg me to forget each one. You say your father swallowed your childhood. His voice. And now he sings forlorn melodies recalling a past he desperately wishes would disappear. He sings late into the night wanting to return. You say you are a wasteland for his memories. Orange-tipped leaves and dry rivers. You say he looks at you and cannot help himself, can only look at you and not say the words.

One morning you tell me your world back home is not as green as I imagine.

I wanted to tell the story of the day Mai put my finger there.

Her touch, so delicate, she could rub two droplets of rain together and make fire. Mai's stories, so fragile, they nearly disappeared on the very tip of her tongue. Her feet, tiny blue butterflies, caressing my ankles, waking me from dreams.

Precocious windowpanes.

My body is absent, so we wait for it to arrive. Mai says she is excited, intrigued by the possibilities of this appearance. We live in twilight. We have conversations in the middle of the night.

I have learned this much from Mai's wisdom: When desire does not hear you, it is better to be silent. By doing violence to the ear, you lose music. Siren songs carried over the whitewater, words nearly drowned by the rhythm of Satan's Cesspool. Caught by this delirium of river language.

Torn away from the place that gives place to her.

On the edge of the South Fork, she seeks the secret of her birth and of her desires. From between her lips come stories so ancient they have nearly disappeared into those deep green jungles, a warm glowing light comes out of her self-embrace and becomes visible.

Once, one single time and one instant only: beauty. Afterwards, or by repetition, there are veils.

Unless.

And what, I ask Mai, if this does not mean anything in your language?

Just like a real photograph, Mai is both here and not here.

When I first reached toward her body, I felt as if I were reaching for her voice, for the very beginnings of her voice through the trees in Vietnam. Not just the sound of her voice, the place of her voice or the making of her voice, but her voice itself.

I become a silent boy trapped by a childhood that cannot be remembered.

Her careful, patient tenderness for this complicated boy.

I want a sentence for my body.

I want my body in a sentence.

I want to be placed tight into this sentence. To learn inside this sentence of your body.

I want to find a sentence that in the making becomes a resurrection. Our skin marked by the remains of language from childhood dreams near the river. The Allegheny. The Monongahela. The Ohio. This trinity of cold rivers that demand that we never forget to forgive. We rub our languages against each other. She just wants. "I desire you." I scrutinize the writing of her body. Search her body, no longer afraid.

A sentence cannot pleasure itself, except unexpectedly.

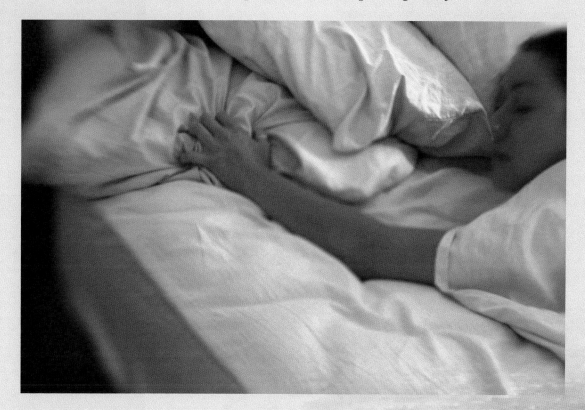

I want to speak to Mai in words, with words, that only have an auditory sense. Words that vibrate against her skin. To speak trembles.

Water obeys water.

While sleeping, Mai's breathing is so gentle that butterflies rest on her belly. But now, Mai no longer sleeps with such stillness. White moonlight floods our bed. Her twisted body. Her feet kick at the sheets. "I am being pulled in too many directions. Torn apart by living." Each delicate blue butterfly flies off into the night.

"I won't say I love you. I just won't. I can't. I don't want my love for you to leave any scars on my tongue, on the roof of my mouth, on the insides of my throat. I can love you without saying this. I like these other ways we have for marking each other, the ways I mark your skin and the ways you mark mine. Freckled parchment. Lines on our backs. Cut wrists. Blistered lips. But I don't want to risk scarring you by saying I love you. Me having said these words to you, I fear, might leave marks on your skin, in your muscles or near your eyes. Seeing this marking would make me sad. I want you to remember me without pain. Years from now, I want for you to be near some river and feel my hand land with the touch of a butterfly on your back between your shoulder blades. That's all. No pain. No brokenhearted nostalgia mumbled to therapists and to friends. Just a tiny, light touch."

Her heart was filled with the sound of a frightened butterfly.

With Lan, I travel to the South Fork of the Yuba River. She says I need new water. We put our feet deep into this strong river, the whitewater nearly pulling us down and under. She opens an old sacred Book of a Voice. A family book listened to in forests, in jungles, in camps waiting for a boat, a way to leave and to arrive, a book listened to in old days before the heart breaks. A book that is a voice with no writing, a book that is a book with no words, a book that is only a voice. A book Lan's family holds inside their breath. As each story is given a voice, we begin walking between origins, between the beginnings of our kinship. We speak only words that have been eroded by the rain and by our hands, by our touch, hesitant, meeting only to erase what once was felt, what once was known, what once could only be whispered among Manzinitas. Innocent habits of children playing along the river.

In the time before the moon waxes red, Alice lived with her very old, nearly speechless mother inside a small wisteria-covered cottage on the furthest outskirts of town. After the sun fell down behind the crest of the hills every evening, Alice's mother wandered through the tiny rooms of their cottage bumping into walls, knocking into chairs and tables. She did this instead of dreaming. She did this instead of resting. She did this while her small daughter lay in her bed exhausted from doing chores.

Inside this cottage, Alice's mother had grown so tired and so terrified of the dark that she rarely ever risked closing her eyes. Even on the brightest of days she lit candles in every room. "To see," she told Alice. "Just to see that there is still light. That light survives." The shadows from these candles gradually took over the house, pushing Alice and her mother into lonely, quiet corners.

Alice's father no longer lived inside this house. He disappeared one night long, long, long ago, while the moon was full. He fled. Ran. Never looked back. He went nowhere. Just gone from sight. People of the village said a runaway dog, a rabid dog, had bitten him. They told tales on street corners of Alice's father growing hair on the palms of his hands. "His eyebrows," they whispered, "so full and so bushy, had grown together." Rumors had it that he abandoned his home because he had begun to fear looking into his young daughter's eyes. Feared what he might see. Feared, more, what she might recognize in his eyes. Or so these stories go. In springtime, more tales of Alice's father emerged from the deep forest. On the quiet night when her father abandoned his desires, Alice slept, flooded by dreams of traveling to some unknown home. As her father set out into the dark forest, she stayed inside these dreams walking alongside rivers, big and strong, in a world filled with light, a place where small girls smelled of lavender and rosemary, a place where shadows could no longer threaten such girls.

Years later, after her father became merely stories whispered by nearly dead old men on street corners when they saw Alice walking through the old, broken town, years after he became merely stories of some forgotten tenderness that floated through her window in the early evening between the hither and thither of dusk and night, Alice began seeing spots of blood in strange places. On the greenest of leaves, on the wettest of river rocks, on the roots of weeping willow trees, Alice saw tiny circles of blood, perfect, nearly invisible, tiny circles. Once she pulled a pomegranate from its branch and fingerprints of this blood appeared on the skin of the dull red fruit. This strange darkness appeared just for a moment, then within a breath, disappeared without leaving a trace. The next day, leaves turned brown, the soil in the garden dried and turned orange, children stopped playing, rain abandoned the village.

One night, before dreams settled into her sleep, Alice saw what appeared to be a reflection of her own body beginning to bleed. Strange blood marked the dead center of her palm. A drop fell onto the earth.

The next morning, barefooted, Alice plopped down out of her bed onto the damp, cold, dirt floor. She would leave before the sun rose over the big black walnut trees. Without a word to her mother, she packed a wooden basket with delicate fruit and little cakes. Beneath these cakes she hid the ancient knife of her nearly forgotten ancestors, this desire to protect herself from her own fears.

She walked out the front door. She needed to be careful with her footsteps. Dreams of her grandmother, a woman of the forest living in a cabin without heat, without light, without water haunted her. Alice had never seen her grandmother; she only heard stories of the life her grandmother once lived in a long-ago past. On this morning, accompanied by these dreams that lingered near her window, Alice disappeared into the fog.

She turned and looked over her left shoulder one final time at the house her father had built. The homestead of her mother. Then, breathing in the cold air, Alice entered the forest. Her calloused feet broke twigs but they did not bleed. Her lips parted, became wet. Her eyes, small, with ancestral words scribbled beneath her eyelids, peered out into the forest, as it grew larger and larger and larger. Alice found her way among the old oak and birch trees, feeling the green, damp moss, down and down the trail to the river. Water over rocks, she followed the sound, knelt at the edge of this lonely river and washed the sins of an old memory from her hands. Cleaned the sins forced on her by the fear of seeing herself suffer. She scrubbed her face with the smallest of pebbles, ones that had been rubbed smooth by year after year of river water. She wished for her skin to fall off her bones into the river. She wished for her soul to be clothed only by moonlight and ferns. She tried to return. In what seemed like another life to Alice, in the time after the time before, one of the elders from the village told her to never leave infancy. That words were perversions of breath, violent deceptions that ruptured silence. Words could only offer false hopes.

Alice came to speech so late in her life that her parents nearly panicked. Waiting. They waited and waited for her to break into the silence. The truth of Alice's stillness frightened her parents. The tender truth of her body, the careful truth of her touch. Alice housed her words, kept them locked in her throat. Held onto them in the red places where blood begins. Instead of entering into speech recklessly, she danced. The tips of her fingers in subtle movements, the flicker of her hand, the slow awakening of her toes. Her torso closer to the movement of river water than any word anyone could ever say. Alice's body kept the promises spoken in this dance. Her first words came when the lilacs bloomed. She spoke of a desire to travel inside out.

"I can't remember things as I used to," Alice said while sitting, in the time after her infancy, near the feet of her parents. "What happens to all the words once you have said them? Where do they go?" Alice feared words were merely being recycled without a thought of their origins. She feared that people simply put them into their mouths and said them carelessly. Said them as if the words did not have origins, as if they had not been born through pain and desires. "I think too many people are talking. There is just too much." Then she fell into the quiet. She spoke no more. Not another word for nearly five years. She smiled up at her parents. Her mouth round and a bit strange for a girl so young. And she retreated again with joy into her palace of forgotten words.

Alice's longing for journeys without language, journeys with only breath and hope, began before her birth. Her body carried markings from some previous life, some other home. The midwife told Alice's parents that Alice was an old child. "Your daughter has the soul of an ancient river. Her body," the midwife said, "has visited this place, here, in the time before." From the very beginning, through the waters of her birthing, Alice learned her desire to abandon her mother.

Since the time of her birth, Alice's right eye had been scarred by what appeared to be a map. Not so much a birthmark as something older, more indefinite. Unclear. Now, in this deep forest, she peered down into the reflection of this map on the surface of the river. She tried to find a way to get beneath the water to see the mapping from behind, to uncover the path beneath the canopy of trees leading to her grandmother's house. But she could not see what she desired to see. She only saw the landscapes of her own uncertainty, landscapes troubled by the impossible. She blinked her eye and the reflection of the map changed. The river flowed and the reflection changed again. The sunlight fell through the branches of the oak trees onto the river, and again the map changed. There was nothing stable about this map, about Alice's broken eye. Paths multiplied and appeared endless and without direction. In this fever of seeing so many angles and diversions, Alice began to think of her words, the words she kept housed in her body. Words of tender magic. Near the river, she enjoyed talking in ways that she had never been able to enjoy back in the village. Here beside this river, her words in this isolation did more than give her solace; her words here, in this place, became rooted. Certain. Her words drew the wonder of the forest toward her. This closeness to the matter of the earth. With each word it was as if the forest entered into her in some physical way. What Alice said in this place endured. Words became dreams, and she remembered. And she kept this remembering with her. From inside this remembering of a future, she traveled with greater faith. "To Grandma's house," she whispered just loud enough for the trees and the river to hear, to know. Words, languages, can be known, trusted, experienced, when devotion is not forgotten. These words clustered around the manzanita trees. The flow of the river carried these words into being, giving birth to a world that existed outside of doubt.

"I am weary of my father trying to protect me. His departure without hope."

Alice rose from the edge of the river, mud fell from her knees. Her feet, she believed, would know the path that would carry her through her own fears to her grandmother's, and she promised not to stray. Leaving her sins, her mad nightmares of a disappeared father, the memory of opening a locked door and seeing that which can never be seen, not with eyes, leaving these sins in the mud on the bank of the river to be cleaned away by the whitewater, she moved her body down the narrow trail.

In the shadows, behind the trees, she heard voices. Promises of flowers more beautiful than any girl had ever known, even in dreams. Flowers beyond imagination. These deep voices longed for Alice to wander. They closed in on her, came near to her breathing. In them, she felt the old days prior to her birth. The days in her mother's womb when her father told stories to the inside. This loveliest of gardens. The place where there was no difference between water and words. The place where water met words. The slip.

"In there, I spoke to you, Mother."

"I am fearful." These words were merely an echo from some far away land. Not her voice. "I would be savage with you."

Alice stared into the spaces between the trees.

"I am fearful I would be savage with you." Alice knew these words. This sound. A hurt down deep. The voice of her father searching his way back to her. "Look here."

Alice stumbled over hearing this voice. She could not look, could not see. Questioned how the voice spoke to her. She found herself on a path that had been grown over. Blackberry bushes and star thistle cut at her ankles. Walking. A man appeared. Or something quite like a man. She tried not to want. But the joy of his eyes confused her. The light that gathered around him clung to his skin and nearly blinded Alice. He stood among white lilies and deep red roses. The roses seemed to bleed onto his skin and turn orange. She knew so very little of what he wanted her to desire.

He broke a flower from its stem. This flower had no name, had never been captured before, had never before been touched by a human hand. Reaching across years, he handed this flower over to Alice. A spasm of years. The flower seemed to join Alice's breathing to a memory of her mother. "Come home. This is too dangerous of a journey." She held the flower between her fingers. A line of blood awakened inside her. Alice nearly cut her skin open in the holding of this flower, tight so tight in her hand. In a moment, if she were not careful, she would bleed. Alice dropped the flower onto the floor of the forest where it immediately took root and blossomed.

"I live inside dreams," the man whispered to her through the branches of the trees. Through the subtle breeze his words appeared before Alice.

"But I," Alice seemed to begin saying, "am not dreaming. Not now. You are not inside my dreaming." "Where are you going?"

"To Grandmother's." The deeper she looked into the man the more he disappeared. But, still, he remained. Stood before her. "The old cabin in the center of the forest belongs to my grandmother. I am going there."

"Wait here. Stay here for this day to pass."

"I will," Alice replied. "I will."

The man separated himself from Alice and walked down the trail away from her toward the deeper center of the forest, disappearing from her sight toward Grandma's house. Alice bent over and reached her hand into the wild flowers and wild herbs—the lotus, the morning glories, the sage, the peppermint—everything mingled together so that there was no way to distinguish one plant from the other. With each flower that she touched, Alice became more tired. Sleepy girl on this precipice where there was blood and knowledge.

"I am becoming marked. Tainted by innocence," Alice whispered. Blackberry stains worked their way into the very center of the palm of her hand. These stains became a kind of salve, a way for protecting her from being cut by other plants. At times, thorns scratched her skin but no blood appeared. Her body held back her bleeding. Alice remained in the present but longed to return to the moment before this present had begun. She believed that her father would return to her. She spent the day in this garden, picking flowers and herbs for her grandmother. And she listened to the breeze moving among the branches. In this dance, this subtle movement of leaves, Alice heard again her father's voice reaching toward her. But she could not make out his words. She only heard the moment before speech. Her father's held breath beneath his skin waiting to awaken words of his desires. His forgiveness.

"Because of you, I live without living within myself."

Alice had never before heard these words, not in this order. She had never before said such words. Perhaps they belonged to her father. Perhaps to her grandmother. Perhaps her mother. Or perhaps the words were merely a way for understanding an arrival and a departure. A weaving together of impossible longing.

This day passed slowly for Alice. And when night finally began to fall on the forest she followed a familiar path of white moonlight toward Grandma's house. Her feet had traveled over these stones in some past life. An old following of abandoned desires. Each step felt like a return, not so much a turning back or even so much of an intentional movement into a memory; it was more like time had become disjointed and this return, this journey, took her down into herself, into those moments of her earliest childhood days before her father left. She felt her father walking beside her. Imagined he whispered to her.

As she walked down this path, she recalled her life as it had once happened. In this place of memory, her father opened a door. Without a sound. Without even the smallest of movements. The morning after her father's escape, a pool of tears appeared on the doorstep. "Don't step in this. Don't," her mother warned her, "it needs to disappear." Mother and daughter stayed locked inside their house. This was the beginning of the lighting of candles. They did not venture outside for days. They sat. They waited. They slept. They waited and they waited. Alice's mother paced. Her feet rubbed raw by the dirt floor. Her hands torn open by her own clawing at what once was there. And they continued to wait and to wait in silence. No speech entered the house; no words were spoken between mother and daughter. Only their bodies without Alice's father. And some mournful breeze that sounded like remnants of a long-forgotten language, words that sounded like they came from the shadows cast by the candlelight, words that made their way through the house coming nearer and nearer to Alice's skin, to her way for remembering.

"Carry the marking of this loss to the river."

Her mother, then, finally said something that could not be heard. Something about the pool of tears, about footprints. Alice looked out the window and saw that there were footprints that appeared to be disappearing. They were muddy footprints but it had not rained for weeks. Her father promised her: "I will not leave you until I leave." A father's promise. "Meet me where the footprints end." She followed these footprints that her father had worn into the forest. A path. Fossils of her father's disappearance. Wordless, she trusted this sense of movement. Even the unpredictable turns in the path, like trapdoors, felt honest. Her father's touch on this path was light. A dream she forgot to dream to the end, one that lingered near her flesh.

Off in the mysterious distance she saw a glimmer of her arrival. A fleck of moonlight bounced off Grandma's windowpane. She thought that she might frighten her grandmother by tapping on her door at such a late hour in such deep darkness, so Alice laid her body down beneath an old, old black walnut tree to rest until sunrise. Brittle branches close to breaking. She slept under this uncertain tree and dreamt dreams of dreaming. Dreamt dreams of her father's eyes. Dreamt dreams that summoned her to open, to spread her fingers. This place where she could once again welcome a return.

"You haven't vanished." Some foreign truth from the time before spilled into her dreams. Tiny pieces of wild stars slipped through her closed eyelids. Even in her dreams Alice lived in the present. If only she could pour these dreams out onto the earth, to grow truth in mud. The mud her father once upon a time rubbed from her skin. He made the wet mud disappear from her young body so that she would be clean, always clean. Only her naked flesh was exposed to the rain falling from the skies. Cleansing. But the mud remained with her father. Marked him. It soiled her father's hands. His touch. She remembered how carefully he smiled. Slow, so as not to break. A care like the care she took when she stepped into the forest to arrive near this place. This following. Here. "I am here."

Her father did not appear to be frightened in her dreams. I beg of you. Fingers that stray absently are dangerous to a daughter's faith. Alice's father kept his fingers still. Even in these dreams that reinvented truth, her father was nearly motionless. Her father only visited her through sound. He became a sound that reached her beneath the doubt of words. The hum of her father's voice caressed her dreams and settled into her bones. And she dreamt these dreams all through the night, on the verge of waking.
These dreams shrunk in the light of the sun falling through the leaves onto her eyelids. In this early dawn she woke beneath a covering of branches and leaves. "I feel like tears." To say what she felt and not what others had taught her

to say. To pass through the limits of feeling and discover a word that had been discarded years and years ago before emotions were sentenced. And to breathe this word into her, to experience this one word in her body. Her father appeared in this breath. Her body rose from slumber and began remembering.

She was careful with the way that she entered the world surrounding her grandmother's house. Alice's body moved among the plants, the trees, the tiny pebbles of the path leading to Grandma's door. A knock. Just one. Slow but deliberate. The door opened. Her feet stepped over the threshold. A shadow passed behind her. The chill of morning on her skin.

"What big, big, big eyes you have," Alice found herself saying.

"To see you," a voice rose from beneath the covers.

Alice did not want to be seen. Wanted only for her body to be held inside her father's dreams. "I wish for you not to see me. Not like this. Not in these ways." Alice tried to cover her dreams behind her eyes. "What strange markings," she said to her grandmother, "on your skin."

"Years of longing."

"Your hands," Alice said. "So large. I am afraid they will break this tiny fruit, these small cakes."

"My knuckles are swollen from years of tending to my garden. My joints are tired. Crippled by this pain.

Feed me, Alice, from your gentle fingers."

Alice felt fear, seeing these scars. Her own hands would once day crack like these hands before her. She feared such marks of kinship. She wanted to escape her grandmother's decaying skin.

"Come closer," Grandma urged Alice. "Be near me."

She walked to the edge of her grandmother's bed and placed the basket on the floor. "I do not understand your body, Grandma."

From beneath the covers, Grandma's words were hollow and echoed. Her breathing was choked. There was no way to escape this weight. Belief, in this place, was never anything more than a shadow.

Alice looked off into the distance, out the window, following the voices in the trees, toward the words that she wanted to say. She rummaged around her small, narrow body. Alice nearly cut herself on these new movements. She felt this changing. A moment that beckoned her to a time away from the time before. She held fast to the slipping away of the past. She needed to rid her body of this demon—the present tense—the moment that flees. "I long to be there behind this reflection. To know a path by touch." To live inside stillness. Alice wanted to sit near the slowest bend of the river. This place where water gathers and holds, a place of waiting on rocks.

"You are no longer this infant girl you were once upon a time in those olden days. You have already become a new girl, a girl who can no longer not know. You cannot deny your body."

Alice imagined one tear falling. Imagined how the river would carry this tear. "My body," she whispers, "is being torn."

"Throw your clothes into the fire, Alice."

"Such big teeth, Grandma. Pointed. So sharp. They look like they would cut through bone."

"Closer. Lie beside me. Bring me your warmth."

Alice stepped toward her grandmother's embrace. Her body so very, very, very small. She became this girl who awaits waiting, a turn back toward a faraway beginning. "I am tender inside all of this that hurts me. You are making me hurt." This man, not quite a man, this man from beside the river—not her grandmother but in her grandmother's nightdress—opened the secrets of disguise, the deceit of words. He wanted her. His breath too hot on her forehead. Alice squirmed, twisted her body. She saw the darkness in what had once upon a time been her grandmother's eyes. Saw the absence of her grandmother there in the place where she was no longer. And from the fireplace she heard ancestral cries. A tuft of hair burning and burning and burning. Always burning.

She waited, anxious, for her dreams to return her to sleep. "I live my life in my dreaming." But this beast lay beside her. This beast wanted nothing more than to devour her. The stink of his desire. Her neck wet with his saliva. Her skin feverish with his breath. This beast wanted to pull the bleeding from Alice. To begin. She had ventured too far away from her mother, had lingered too long in the forest, had wandered away from the path. She had been told to follow. Her mother told her the journey to Grandma's was a litany. "Your feet will know to follow the old words scurrying like autumn leaves upon the forest path." Listen. Alice never gave up this believing in the whispering that haunted the spaces between the trees, the whispering of her father in the leaves of these trees.

She resisted the anger that boiled in the blood of this demon, the raw yellow blood in his eyes. The beast pawed at her thighs. Pulled at her skin. Wanted to peel her skin away from her bones. This tug. She felt only like fleeing. Like fleeing from what she had been told to believe, fleeing from all that this world could offer. To show her father that she did not fear him and that he need not fear her. That in the forest—beneath the rocks, near the river, under the skin of the leaves—words still could hold truth. She found those places, the sacred places, and he would be safe and he could stay. Not leave. "I will find my way back to you because I know how to allow myself to wander like a stray leaf."

Halfway between her faith and her splintered dreaming, Alice struggled to lift her body away from the ugly words that soiled this unholy bed of her grandmother. Alice knew that her grandmother had been disappeared into the traps beneath the skin of this beast and that she had died in this skin. And Alice knew she needed to fear, knew that her death also waited for her under the skin of this old sinner. Her grandmother, she knew, could no longer be called back, could no longer save her.

The beast wanted only to touch her. Told her that his touch would save her. His one touch, this one touch, he said, would make her pure. You will be made unvirgin. A lone voice from the spaces between the trees. A howling voice carried by the wind. A secret child's desire that was yet to be unveiled. But Alice was somebody who had never been a mirror, had never needed the protection of a bolted door. She closed her mouth. Her lips tight. The beast told Alice that she needed to abandon waiting. "Time will destroy you if you try to remain still." This unbroken girl knew nothing of words that had been stolen from the safety of her skin. She knew only the murmur of water over rocks at the edge of the river, knew only how to pull words back down toward her skin, the caress of water over rock. This home for words. She disturbed silence, spoke, only when she needed to forget her body, to slip beneath the desires of this beast, spoke only to sidestep the inevitable cutting of time into her flesh. But she refused to believe in time. She knew only that time was, that time had once—long, long, long ago—been but that time would be no longer. Her sentences were filled with ways to escape time, filled with forgetfulness and ways for getting lost in delirious scenes that lingered near her eyes.

If only her father could step back into this movement, could say one single word into this place; breathe one syllable into her memory. If only his photograph could appear before her, beside her, could emerge from her skin, his skin visible through her skin. Pain of such memories of her father opened her heart. This past that has never been present, this past that could never be. But she became lost to the world of her father and she was left in a circle of desire exceeding its boundaries in every direction. Stranded. Without home. Loss was a word just as Alice herself was a girl like a word near the river. She needed to forge her own body into this present.

The beast placed his mouth near her neck. But Alice unloosed her tongue. Beneath this skin you so desire are hidden flames, joyous torments, cruel wounds, sweet bitterness. Word after word fell from her hands. Each word grew larger and larger and larger as she placed them into the world. Alice wanted to exist with words without turning them into sentences. A sentence renders time. She desired only to loosen her tongue without following what was born of her tongue. Alice covered this torrential pouring forth of words with unspoken speaking. This birth of breath. Round words that enchanted the large white moon. Her mouth opening and opening; her body talking and talking until there were no more tongues for talking. A mouthful of lyrical desertions. "Here. Touch me here."

Nothing stays.

But the beast could not understand words uttered from a girl who escaped time. And he brought his hurried paw toward her eyes. Alice turned cold and quiet. Fascinated by the hesitation behind his touch so near to her skin, the voice in her throat, she held her breath down deep in her womb. Held breathing tight to the place where her desires began. Her body wandered near to the dark secrets of her tears. She was alone, burning, with this long ago sin, the sin from before her birth. She reached over the edge of her bed down into her basket. She pulled the ancient knife of her kin from beneath the cakes she had packed in the early light of the morning and in one lonely swift motion she put an end to this beast. There was a small, narrow trickle of blood, then careful silence. Not a word spoken. Alice wanted for her whole body to escape the impossibility of words, wanted for her whole body to be necessary. Trees outside her grandmother's window calmed themselves of their desires.

Alice would remain in this house where her grandmother once lived. In the morning she washed the sheets and hung them out to dry on the clothesline in the wild forest breeze. Blood always disappears. She grew old in this house and never saw her mother again. She spent her days, day after day, searching for her father along the paths around her grandmother's house. She sought his voice, followed the appearance of his voice into the deep green forest down to the river and she sat near the water. She followed her father into her dreams, until, exhausted, she hunted no more and settled into the quiet of her grandmother's front porch and waited.

And waited. She waited. And she waited. With each breath.

Mai wanted every bruise she carried from what she could not forget to become miracles.

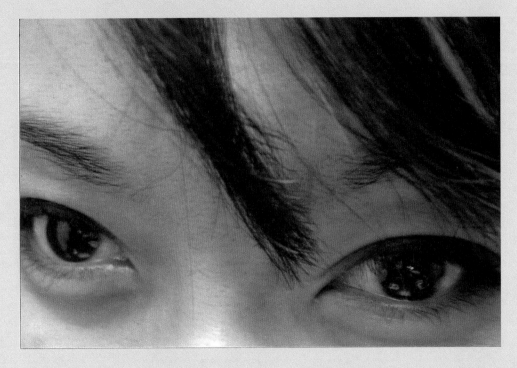

I learned to write her name without moving. To write Mai's name while sitting perfectly still. Farsighted, I worked so close to the page that I began to forget the space between my desire, this pencil, and her body, this page. Writing her name became near to touching her again.

Last night on the phone you could not remember. You had forgotten how long it had been. How many years had passed. You said fourteen years. Then you said, "No, longer. It has been longer, more years have passed." Then, then, you said, less. You said, less, it has been less. I nearly corrected you. It has been eighteen years. That night when it rained. That night when the rain never stopped. September in Sacramento. You're there. Home. I am in the foothills. Your voice travels to me through the phone, through this distance. I could never trust telephones. What the wires do to voices. The breaking down of voices to a long series of abstract numbers, not even letters. Tiny dancers. But with you, it was different. Your voice somehow escaped that. I could hear skin in your voice even through the phone. I waited. You said these stories must exhaust me. It's one o'clock in the morning. You say that I need to rest. Sleep. Dream.

Your voice carried with it the force of myth.

Years ago Kathy always called in the middle of the night. Once she called every night for three weeks or so and read Juan Goytisolo's *Solitary Bird* to me. Her body in San Francisco. Mine in Ohio. Her voice so raw as if she were speaking from the very origins of language, of desire. "You'll love this story," she said. And I listened to her, thinking at first that she was just making up a fairytale. A lullaby from the Bay. Kathy always became afraid in the night, of the night. Lonely and desperate. Longing. I told Craig, "Kathy's reading me bedtime stories." She cried when she read them. Her vague longing to be somewhere else in time while holding to the present. The never of always.

Mai says she feels like she is a tree in late autumn the moment after it has dropped its last leaf.

From Viet Nam, Mai writes. Water lives in language here.

And I want one last time to spoon moonlight between her thin lips.

Standing along the banks of the Yuba with Lan, we make our return to childhood. Trees from mythological tales. The scent of the pomegranate. Blackberry blossoms. The frayed strap of Lan's backpack. Lan hands me a necklace, one that her grandmother had made, one filled with voices and water, a circle, a labyrinth to be worn near my heart. I tell Lan there is nothing obvious about Mai's beauty, that her beauty requires a careful pilgrimage, a long journey to rivers waiting for rains, that this beauty, hers, is listened to through the voice of her stories, is experienced with skin and muscle and memory. A beauty that enters and stays. Lan looks directly into my eyes and says, "You cannot love in secret." Her toes touch the skin of my feet and for one moment I remember Mai. Mornings.

"I do not want to tell a story to someone's memory."

I want to remember. "Nothing I've written here matters. I just want to love—are you listening to me?"

Like a real photograph, both here and no there, both here and not here, Mai and I look, in secret, across the space that separates us from touch, from words, from breath, from muscle.

A slip of time that confuses time.

We retrace our desire with each glance backward into a photograph of the two of us in an embrace. Mai's breath on my neck, my fingers pressed into her spine. In looking at this photograph here in the present, we are repeatedly carried back to that exact moment when it was taken in the past. A past that happened in the before, a past that, now, inside this photograph and with each gaze directed toward this photograph, happens endlessly while the actual moment of that embrace no longer exists even though the photograph itself makes the embrace seem to appear in the present once again.

Years later, this photograph will mark the presence of disappearance.

Forgetting cannot happen except by remembering and there is no remembering without first forgetting.

Holding photographs of you in my hands, here in Lotus, with you far far away traveling through Southeast Asia, my stories become myths, each one beginning beneath a moon that somehow rises in the south and awaits dawn.

I touch the shadows in Mai's hair. Her soft soft words filled with roots.

In Mai, the rivers move. Her scent rooted to the trails of Magnolia and the edge of the South Fork.

Stories were written:

Under her eyelids.

In the stitches that held together her favorite dress.

On the very tip of her fingers.

A moment before sunrise.

Under rocks. On branches that have fallen from trees along the river. On the surface of water.

In moonlight.

She said her thoughts were filled with mirrors.

Our words slipped in and out of water.

Mai writes.

At the end of the day what I wish to tell you and only you I put away because I know you are sad and I am sad and I don't want this sadness to swallow the tiny sentences that matter so much to us. But I am afraid of all these things that tear us, so I will be patient.

Maybe you hate that I say this, that every word is a goodbye. I know you are frustrated with me, this communion, this love, but I cannot move toward that yet. And I don't know if I ever will. I only know that I do not want to be formed by your hands, so I must travel, must go.

You can never own water, really.

Photographs capture the appearance that slips away.

Closed lips guard memory. Veiled eyes. "Everywhere," Lan whispers against my skin, "there is air, which is invisible but always there, here, to touch you, to be touched by you. "

Naked moonlight gathers close to Mai's skin.

This knot of our innocence.

Against my skin, her body lay like soft moonlight.

Mai felt swallowed and lost and was tired of being secret.

It was a Saturday. He was on his way to the post office in Auburn driving out of the canyon when his cell phone rang. They spoke for nearly an hour. She in an airport in San Francisco on her way to Viet Nam. He in a parking lot. They talked until she boarded the plane then she said goodbye. He remembered being ten or so on the shore of Geneva-on-the-Lake, Ohio. He remembered the light wave of the lake pulling down his sand castle. He felt that lonely again.

This deep blue estrangement of our touch.

Because my muscles are tight with longing.

Lan kicks a rock into the Yuba River. She says, "Love needs aroused tranquility."

"Perhaps," Clarice whispers from beneath the moon, from near the river, "to love is to give one's own solitude to others? For it is the very last thing we have to offer."

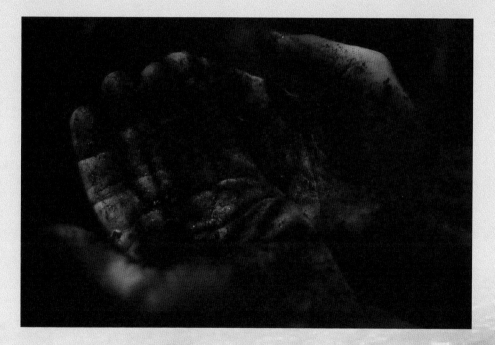

Unable to begin at the beginning, here is the river. It was waiting, here when you were born. Waiting.

Before the moon disappeared, the river began remembering, carrying desire, a longing to return, to find its way home. Rivermuscle on a pilgrimage, knowing, without stopping to learn language becoming language. Pure breath. Men on the weather station say: "The river is flooding." Those who know the river know the river is just remembering, just wanting to go home. So I drive down the hills into the valley toward the bay area with lonely river prophets on my tongue for you. For that one startled bone of your hip. To speak there. In that purple bruise, the bruise you touch with the very tip of your fingers when you look into your mirror.

When anyone reads this but you, it begins to be lost.

When in the night you touch fire, you experience the boundaries of your day. You separate this fire from its flame in a distant mirror. Blurred. There before breath, before water, before your hand covers your mouth, you capture a glimpse of a photograph burning, and you remember a moment filled with impulse and birth, still vibrant with life. It is that Friday before you pack to leave for San Francisco. This almost imperceptible enclosure of tree branches, of whitewater, of an eclipsed sun. On a riverbank along the South Fork where the moon has been sweating, I listen for the memory of your footsteps and sand.

"But I cannot tell you more. There is a part, a little secret and mysterious, I believe that is for us."

Amber

End Notes

Some of these photographs were at one time authentic, true moments of being. Some were accidents and continue to be accidents of perception. Some were not. A few have been found in family albums and then inserted near my memories or near to Mai's memories. A few photographs verify what letters, words and sentences may have turned into myths. Throughout this narrative some photographs arrest time. Some nearly make visible the moment of the Japanese concept of the "ma", a pause as important as the words, as important as the image. Most often these photographs become an architectural memory of time past— Eliotic moments of time was, time is, time will be again.

A special thank you to Rebecca Woolston and Marie-Anne.

Page 23: *chaque fois que je dis je I je jette un coup d'oeil autour de moi poru voir ou You* is from Helene Cixous.

Page 31: *J'ai toujours aime l'eau passionnement.* From Helene Cixous.

Page 46: *"Khong biet sau nay tui no con nho tieng me de khong?"* from *Tales of Love*, Trinh T. Minh-ha

Page 60: *"Con nghi phai hoa minh voi ngon ngu thi moi duy tri duoc tieng me de."* from *Tales of Love*, Trinh T. Minh-ha

About the Author

Doug Rice was born in Pittsburgh, Pennsylvania. He received his BA in English from Slippery Rock State College, took his MA in creative writing at SUNY-Binghamton, where he studied under John C. Gardner, and his MA in English Literature at Duquesne University. He studied for his PhD in Literature at the University of Pittsburgh. His first novel, *Blood of Mugwump*, was selected by Kathy Acker as a runner-up for the FC2 First Novel Award. He has taught at La Roche College, Kent State University-Salem and currently teaches creative writing, literary theory and film history and theory at Sacramento State University. His work has appeared in numerous anthologies and literary journals including *Avant Pop: Fiction for a Daydream Nation, Dirty : Dirty Anthology, Kiss the Sky, Alice Redux, Phantoms of Desire, Discourse, Gargoyle, Zyzzyvya*, and others. His work has been translated into Polish, Spanish, French, Portuguese and German.

ALSO FROM JADED IBIS PRESS

Aunt Pig of Puglia, a memoir by Patricia Catto. Art by Debra Di Blasi. Audio reading by Patricia Catto.

Burn Your Belongings, a novel by David Hoenigman. Art and music by Yasutoshi Yoshida.

Blank, a novel by Davis Schneiderman. Art by Susan White. Music by Paul D Miller aka DJ Spooky.

Unfinished, short stories finished by Lily Hoang. Art finished by Anne Austin Pearce. Music by Tornado in a Jar aka Ron Heckert, with vocals by Betsy Carney and production by Carlos DeLeon).

Daughter, a novel by Janice Lee. Art by Rochelle Ritchie Spencer. Music by Resident Anti-Hero.

The Vicious Red Relic, Love, a fabulist memoir by Anna Joy Springer. Art by Anna Joy Springer. Music by Anna Joy Springer and Rachel Carns and Tara Jane O'Neil.

The Forests of The Vicious Red Relic, Love, a companion to the fabulist memoir, by Anna Joy Springer. Art by COLOR ART for COLOR EDITION: Original art by Teresa Carmody & Maude Place, Rachel Carns, Paula Cronin, Kristie Fleming, Shelley Jackson, Cristy C. Road, beldAn Sezen, Rhani Remedes and Aron Cometbus, Leon Mostovoy, Tara Jane O'Neil, Anna Joy Springer, Annie Sprinkle & Beth Stephens (Love Art Lab), and Miriam Klein Stahl.

No One Told Me I Was Going To Disappear, a novel by J. A. Tyler (text) and John Dermot Woods (images). Music by John Gallaher.

We: a reimagined family history, a novel by c.vance. Art by Debra Di Blasi. Music by Patch Rubin.

Glamorous Freak: How I Taught My Dress To Act, a novel by Roxanne Carter. Photography by Roxanne Carter. Music by Megan Body.

The Pornographers, a novel by Christopher Grimes; **Pornographies**, short stories by Christopher Grimes. Art by Scott Zieher Smith. Music by OCnotes and Lisa Dank.

Joyful Noise: for three or more voices, poems by Mathew Timmons.

The Secret Life of Objects, a memoir by Dawn Raffel. Art by Sean Evers.

Family Romance, a novel by Nick Patters (visuals) and Tom Bradley (verbals).

Waiting Up for the End of the World, poetry by Elizabeth J. Colen. Art by Guy Benjamin Brookshire.

Book of Knut: a novel by Knut Knudson, a novel by Halvor Aakhus. Art by Halvor Aakhus.

Dirty : Dirty, an anthology of dirty art and writing. Art by Mugi Takei. Writing by Greg Bachar, Elizabeth Burns, Jennifer Calkins, Jane L. Carman, Kylee Cook, Beth Couture, Dirk Cowan, Justin Dobbs, Trevor Dodge, C. M. Connelly, April Gigliotti, Christopher Grimes, Steve Halle, Jeff Hansen, Michael Harold, Garrett Hayes, Jacqueline Heffron, Lily Hoang, Nabila Najwa, Eric Jeitner, Liesl Jobson, Steve Katz, Kimberly Koga, Stacey Levine, Marilyn Jaye Lewis, Robert Lopez, Cris Mazza, Joe Milazzo, Kathleen Miller, Scott Million, Theresa A. O'Donnell, Jordan Okumura, Melanie Page, Mitch Parker, Aimee Parkinson, Jack Rees, AE Reiff, Doug Rice, Heather Hendrix Russell, Thaddeus Rutkowski, Davis Schneiderman, Mikal Shapiro, Gary Shipley, Ascot Smith, Rob Stephenson, Helen Tran, Holms Troelstrup, J. A. Tyler, c.vance, Laura Vena, Hal Wert, Lane Williams, Alyssa Wisener, Rion Woolf, and Lidia Yuknavitch.

Imago for the Fallen World, poems by Matthew Cooperman and art by Marius Lehene.

visit us for more smart books
jadedibisproductions.com

22123489R00134

Made in the USA
Charleston, SC
11 September 2013